The
Big Play

**Vivid accounts of nineteen memorable
NFL games in which one dramatic "big
play" made or broke a champion team.**

RANDOM HOUSE / **NEW YORK**

The Big Play

By Harold Rosenthal

ILLUSTRATED WITH PHOTOGRAPHS

Manufactured in the United States of America

Designed by Peter Schaefer

Photograph credits: Vernon J. Biever title page, 64, 92, 110, 113, 136–137, 140, 147, 148, 163, 167, 169; Culver Pictures 15, 33; New York Daily News *77, 103; United Press International 5, 7, 10, 18, 26, 32, 35, 38, 45, 70, 83, 87, 90, 95, 99, 150, 158, 173; Wide World 23, 28, 43, 47, 52, 56, 62, 79, 101, 105, 112, 117, 127, 128, 130, 155, 176.*
Cover photographs: James Drake

This title was originally catalogued by the Library of Congress as follows:

Rosenthal, Harold.
　　The big play. New York. Random House [1965]
　　viii, 184 p. illus., ports. 22 cm. (The Punt, pass, and kick library, 3)

　　1. National Football League. 2. Football—Hist.　ɪ. Title.

GV955.5.N35R66　　　　　796.33278　　　　　65—22659

Trade Ed.: ISBN: 394-80193-8　　Lib. Ed.: ISBN: 394-90193-2

Contents

Introduction

The magic of "the big play" is that it can come at any time, in any game. It needs no big star, no special set of circumstances. But after it happens, it stays in the memories of those who witness it.

The National Football League, in its half-century of professional competition, has produced hundreds of big plays. Only a few could be fitted within the covers of this book. If your favorite player has been omitted, you can always feel that his special big play was not overlooked by the most important observer of all—you.

It may have been a pass by a Johnny Unitas, a

kick by a Pat Summerall, a tremendous scoring day by a Paul Hornung, a fumble that bounced the wrong way (or the right way, depending on the spectator's point of view). But almost always the big play remains in the fan's memory long after the details, the supporting players—even the scores— have faded away.

Of course every play in a game could be called a big play because football is a team game, and one play leads to another. A two-yard gain to complete a first down in a scoring march could easily have been as important, and as big, as the spectacular pass which finished it off. Thus, for every hero of a big play there are hundreds of unsung heroes of other contributing plays that made possible the one which stood out.

The great attraction of football is that there will always be new big plays to treasure alongside those of the past. New stars appear to give their best. In the process more big plays are certain to thrill the fans who follow football from the warm days of early September through the icy blasts of December.

On sunlit afternoons, under blazing lights, in downpours, in the grip of winter's frosty fingers, the Big Play is always possible. It is the game's extra bonus to its followers.

The Big Play

1

Chicago Bears vs.
New York Giants
At New York
December 15, 1946

Sid Luckman, the finest high-school and college football player ever developed in New York, was back in his home town. But he was returning at the head of an invading force. Luckman was now playing for the Chicago Bears. And the Bears saw only one obstacle in their path to the 1946 National Football League championship—the New York Giants.

Since graduating from Columbia University in New York City, Luckman had become a great professional star. He fitted perfectly into the quarterback spot in the newly developed T-formation offense of the Bears. But when Luckman had been a college player, Columbia used the single-wing type of offense like most other college teams. In the single wing, the center snapped the ball directly to the tailback. In the T formation, the quarterback moved right up close behind the center, so the exchange of the ball from one to the other was a matter of inches.

From 1940 through 1943 Luckman had quarterbacked the Bears to three victories in four play-off games. However, this 1946 game between the Bears and Giants would be the first title contest in which he could demonstrate his prowess to his old hometown supporters.

It was a cold gray afternoon when the Bears arrived at the Polo Grounds. They were favored to win, and with good reason. Injuries had laid low some of the Giants' first-line players. Bill Paschal, their best fullback, had suffered a broken jaw the week before. And some of the other New York stalwarts were also sidelined on account of physical disabilities. The Giants were definitely the under-

Sid Luckman (42) practices passing during a workout with the Bears.

dogs in this fray.

The spectators at the game were to see football at its roughest. Many players on both teams were just back from World War II service in the armed forces. Apparently they were eager to prove that, even if older, they were still able both to take punishment and to dish it out.

Some of the football "experts" were claiming that Luckman's job was actually easy. Because of the strong pass protection given him by his teammates, they felt he should have been ashamed to accept his salary. No opposing team dared dirty the seat of Sid's pants, a few said sourly. To do so would stir the mighty Bears to such a height of rage that only heaven could help the perpetrators of such a deed.

Such statements didn't exactly reflect the facts. The record showed that during the 1946 regular season Luckman had lost a total of 76 yards while being smeared by onrushing defenders on passing attempts. He had not tried to carry the ball once. His job was to direct the offense, and to pass. Only the Los Angeles Rams' Bob Waterfield had topped Sid in completions and touchdown passes.

The action in the first quarter of the game seemed to portend a rout of the handicapped Giants. First Luckman jolted them with a 21-yard touchdown pass to Ken Kavanaugh, the Bears' lanky end. Then

Chicago Bears vs. New York Giants

Chicago's Dante Magnani intercepted a pass thrown by Frank Filchock, and galloped 37 yards across the goal line for a second Bear touchdown. Frank Maznicki kicked the extra point each time, so the Bears had a quick 14–0 lead.

The Giants, fourteen points behind after the first eight minutes of play, battled back doggedly. With three minutes left in the first period, they put on a 57-yard drive. Filchock capped it by passing to Frank Liebel for 38 yards and a touchdown. Veteran Ken Strong booted the conversion to make the

After intercepting one of Frank Filchock's passes in the second quarter, Dante Magnani (3) is tackled by a Giant.

score Bears 14, Giants 7.

The New Yorkers continued to fight fiercely, and they managed to contain the Bear attack in the second quarter. Neither side scored, so the half ended with the tally still 14–7.

In the third period the Giants got a break when Chicago's Bill Osmanski fumbled. Jim Lee Howell recovered the ball on the Bears' 22-yard line. Chicago was set back farther by a penalty for roughing, after which Filchock carried the ball to the Chicago 5. He tried a pass that missed, then hit receiver Steve Filipowicz with a toss in the end zone. A successful kick by Strong tied the score, 14–14.

The injury-ridden Giants had no good punter available. Howie Livingston, pressed into emergency service, got off a poor kick near the end of the third period. The punt went out of bounds after covering only 16 yards.

The Bears were in possession on their own 29-yard line. They moved to the 34 as the quarter ended. After the final period began, Chicago fought down to the New Yorkers' 19-yard line, helped considerably by a roughing penalty imposed against the Giants. At this point Luckman pulled a surprise. He called for a play the Bears had kept in cold storage all year.

Known in the Chicago play book as "97 Bingo," it called for Luckman to carry the ball after faking a handoff. This he did beautifully, with George McAfee seeming to make a run at the Giants' right end. Luckman, hiding the ball against his hip, raced through a hole in the left side of the New York line. He was getting good blocking from the right side of his own line. He was at the 10-yard line before the Giant defenders realized that Luckman had the ball and closed in on the Bears' flying quarterback. A couple of them hit him at the 5-yard line, but he kept on his feet and finally tumbled, off balance, into the end zone. Maznicki again kicked the extra point. The score: Bears 21, Giants 14.

The Giants were behind, but by a deficit of only seven points. Their situation was seemingly not hopeless. Then, with only five minutes left to play, Maznicki booted a 26-yard field goal, putting the Bears ahead 24–14. And that was the final score of the game.

The statistics of the game showed a surprisingly close performance on offense by the two teams. The Giants outgained the Bears on the ground, 120 yards to 101. The Bears' passing-yardage edge was only 144 to 128. Filchock completed as many forward passes as Luckman, but six of his attempts were intercepted. Only two of Luckman's were

9

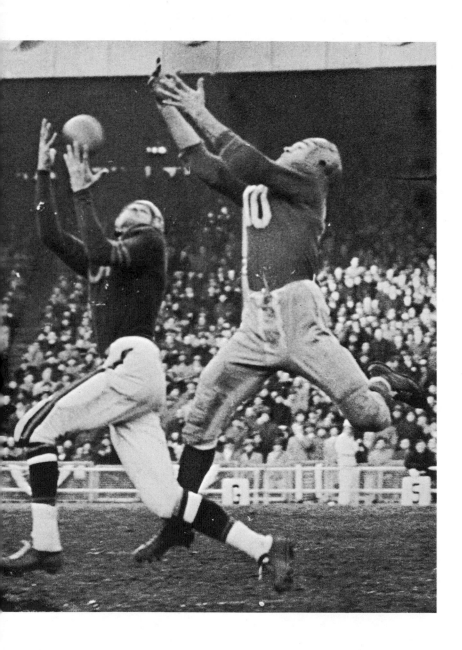

pulled down by his opponents. Sid himself grabbed Filchock's last toss to stop the Giants' final offensive thrust.

It had been a bruising, bone-jarring battle. The Giants' Frank Filchock got a broken nose early in the game but went on playing anyway. Frank Reagan, a fine running back for the New York eleven, was knocked out in the second quarter. George Franck, another ball carrier, wound up in the hospital with a shoulder separation.

Sid Luckman has been retired from gridiron-glory days for many years. But no matter how long he has been out of the game, he is not likely to forget —nor will those who watched it—his one and only ball-carrying feat of 1946. It won a championship for the Bears.

Ken Kavanaugh (left) catches a 25-yard pass thrown by Luckman while Giant Howie Livingston tries vainly to intercept.

2

Chicago Cardinals vs.
Chicago Bears
At Chicago

December 12, 1948

It was cold as only Chicago can be cold in mid-December. The wind whipped off Lake Michigan, across Lake Shore Drive, and swirled its icy fingers around Wrigley Field. There it met the heat generated by the final, exciting clash of the NFL's 1948 Western Division race.

In the second game of the season, the Bears had triumphed over the Cardinals, their Windy City rivals, 28–17. Some planning genius among the League's schedule makers had saved the return clash between the Cards and the Bears—champions and runners-up, respectively, of the year before—for this last Sunday of the regular 1948 season.

During the season, each of these powerhouses had run up a record of ten victories and only one defeat. Whichever team won at Wrigley Field would go on to meet the Eagles a week later in the League play-off.

No matter how they performed against other teams in any given season, the Bears and the Cardinals always went all out when they played against each other. (This was before the Cardinal franchise was moved to St. Louis.) Sometimes their games seemed more like gang fights than football games. But the fans loved them. And more than 51,000 enthusiastic spectators filled every bit of space in Wrigley Field for the decisive contest of 1948.

The Bears were in the process of finding a successor to the great Sid Luckman, who was nearing the end of his career as quarterback. On their roster were Notre Dame's Johnny Lujack and the University of Texas' Bobby Layne.

The Cardinals had at quarterback Paul Christman and Ray Mallouf. Power was the word for the rest of their backfield. Football fans everywhere knew the names and the exploits of Pat Harder, Charley Trippi, Elmer Angsman and Marshall

Sid Luckman (center) and his two successors, Johnny Lujack (left) and Bobby Layne.

Goldberg. The Bears, however, had George McAfee, Mike Holovak, Bill Osmanski and George Gulyanics to counter with.

There were enough heroes to win a dozen games on the field that cold and windy afternoon. Yet a couple of defensive moves by a center and a defensive back had as much to do with deciding the issue as the playing of any passer, runner or kicker.

For three periods, rookie Johnny Lujack kept the Bears out in front. In the first half they limited the

15

Cardinals to a 34-yard field goal, kicked by Harder. Meanwhile, the Bears scored twice, once on Lujack's touchdown pass to Ken Kavanaugh and again when the former Notre Dame star completed one to Gulyanics. The half-time score was Bears 14, Cardinals 3.

In the third quarter, Cardinal back Pat Harder recovered an onside kick by the Bears on the enemy 46-yard line. Four plays later Harder belted through left tackle for a touchdown, after having completed a long pass from Christman. Half-frozen Cardinal fans had their first chance to whoop it up and get their blood circulating. Harder also kicked the extra point, to put his team only four points behind, 14–10.

On the first play of the fourth period, however, Gulyanics scored a Bear touchdown on a short rush. Adding the extra point, the Bears again had an eleven-point bulge—leading 21–10.

Then things began to happen, mostly for the benefit of the Cardinals. With the help of a holding penalty and a pass-interference ruling against the Bears, they marched 85 yards to a touchdown in eight plays. Charley Trippi capped the drive with a 5-yard slash outside left guard that carried him over the goal line. Again Harder made the extra point. The score was Bears 21, Cards 17.

16

Two minutes later, with the Bears on offense, Lujack threw a pass aimed at lanky Ken Kavanaugh. The Cards' veteran defensive center, Vince Banonis, stepped in and picked it off on the Bears' 46. Making his second interception of the year, Banonis ran the ball all the way to the 20 before Bear tacklers hauled him down.

Two plays later, Elmer Angsman shouldered his way across the enemy goal line for a big six-pointer. Then Harder kicked his 53rd consecutive extra point, and the Cards led, 24–21.

With half a period still left, the Bears sent Sid Luckman in at quarterback. A scoring pass was obviously their only hope. Luckman started out as though he would come through for the Bears, as he had so many times in the past. He completed three passes in a row, and the Bear fans came alive. But on his next attempt Sid was smeared for a loss. Doggedly he tried another forward pass. This time he hit his halfback, J. R. Boone, who caught the ball over his shoulder on the Cardinals' 15.

There were only a few minutes of playing time left. If the Bears scored, the Cards probably wouldn't have enough time to retaliate.

Don Kindt, the Bear fullback, took a shot at the line to loosen things up a bit. Then Luckman tried an end-zone pass.

When the ball came down the only man near it was Johnny Cochran, Cardinal defensive back. He grabbed it, slipped as he tried to run, and fell in his own end zone. It was an automatic touchback, giving the Cards possession on their own 20-yard line.

They ran the ends and punched away at the tackles, making 5- and 10- and 2-yard gains. The

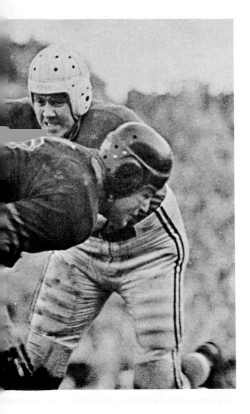

Two Cardinals come up behind Bear back Don Kindt (6), nailing him after he has sprinted 10 yards with the ball.

Bears fumed while the remaining seconds drained from the clock. When the time finally ran out, the Cards were on the Bears' 10. It had been a great exhibition of ball control.

The 24–21 triumph gave the Cards possession of the Western Division crown for the second straight year. The alert defensive plays of Banonis and Cochran had knocked the Bears into second place.

19

3

Philadelphia Eagles vs. Chicago Cardinals At Philadelphia

December 19, 1948

The weather in Philadelphia on Sunday morning, the 19th of December, 1948, offered little encouragement for the big football game to be played that afternoon. People who got up and went out for the Sunday papers found an inch or more of snow already on the ground, and more falling steadily. Some of them commented that it looked as if there would be a white Christmas. Others shrugged and said nothing. It didn't matter much to them, one way or the other.

A third group of people reacted strongly, however. They were the players scheduled to appear in the NFL championship game to be played in Shibe Park. The prospect of snow didn't please either the home-town Eagles or Chicago's visiting Cardinals. Quite the opposite. Snow, or any other unusual weather condition, almost always requires a change in game plans. And no one likes to see a week's preparatory work disappear in a swirling curtain of white.

Game plans weren't the only things that disappeared that afternoon. As the snow continued to blanket the gridiron, it sometimes seemed as if the players themselves would be lost in a snowy wilderness during the progress of the game. They looked liked helmeted wraiths wavering around on an unearthly white-blanketed field.

The Eagles had battled their way to the top of the Eastern Conference with a record of nine victories, two losses and one tied game. In the Western Conference the Cardinals had dropped only one game out of twelve, and had defeated the Bears at Wrigley Field. Steve Van Buren, Philadelphia's great running back, was the NFL's leading ground gainer. Likewise, the Eagles' quarterback, Tommy Thompson, led the League with 25 touchdown passes during the regular season.

Two days before the big game, four players on the Eagles squad work out on the field: (left to right) Bosh Pritchard, Tommy Thompson, Joe Muha, and Steve Van Buren.

The Chicagoans had chalked up a total of 395 points, a top record in the League and convincing evidence of the Cards' scoring punch. Cardinal stars Pat Harder and Mal Kutner were first and second, respectively, in the individual-player point-scoring department.

Shibe Park's capacity was 36,000 and all seats had been sold well in advance of the game. The Cardinals had beaten the Eagles in the previous year's play-off. The Eagle fans, firmly convinced that their 1948 team was one marked by destiny, had waited long for this day.

It was therefore unfortunate that, when the day arrived, it was better suited for skiing than for football. The not quite 29,000 hardy folk actually in the stands at game time wore all types of Arctic-weather gear. A few minutes after they occupied their snow-laden bleacher seats, their garments, too, had turned white, merging into the background.

The game began half an hour late. A ninety-man crew had labored three hours shoveling snow off the canvas that covered the playing field. As the big covering was rolled away, the fans cheered at the sudden appearance of the great green rectangle in the surrounding whiteness.

Their joy was short-lived. The snow kept on pelting down. In ten minutes the freshly uncovered field was as white as its surroundings. Sidelines, yard lines and goal lines all had vanished.

Hastily the crew set up markers along one side of the field. Sticks erected in heaps of snow signified 10-yard intervals. Red flags marked each goal line, with two more flags showing the boundary of the end zone. The teams agreed on an essential ground rule for yardage—all decisions by referee Ron Gibbs would be final. Only once during the game did officials have to resort to measurement.

Passing seemed to be virtually out of the question. Still, on the first play after the Eagles took possession, Quarterback Tommy Thompson audaciously heaved a long throw from his own 35-yard line. Jack Ferrante, a Philadelphia end, caught it over his shoulder on the Chicago 20. Two Cardinals hit him, but he managed to keep on his feet and ran the ball for a touchdown.

The play was called back. The Eagles had been offside. The fans' excited roar changed to a muffled groan.

In the second period, the Eagles had two more chances to score. The first time, they recovered a Cardinal fumble on the Chicago 21-yard line. Two Philadelphia passes missed fire, however, and the Cardinals intercepted a third one. Later in the quarter, the Eagles reached the 8-yard line before Cliff Patton missed a 15-yard field-goal attempt.

Scoring obviously was going to be as difficult for both teams as it had been easy for the Cardinals in the regular season. When the first half came to an end neither side had made a tally of any kind.

During the third quarter, the opposing forces churned back and forth, equally unable to mount a scoring threat. Then Ray Mallouf, the Cardinal

quarterback, fumbled the ball just as the period was
about to end.

Frank Kilroy, an Eagle guard, was alert and
made the recovery for Philadelphia on the Chicago 18-yard line. Bosh Pritchard, halfback, moved
the ball to the 12 on the next play. The officials
signaled the end of the quarter and the ball was
moved to the other end of the field.

Joe Muha next carried the ball for four yards.
Then Tommy Thompson himself sneaked inside
tackle for two more.

Bosh Pritchard (right) is tackled after gaining 5 yards for the Eagles.

"Give it to Steve!" The muffled roar sounded from the snowbound stands.

Thompson did give it to Steve (Van Buren) on the next play. Van Buren cradled the ball close and hit off right tackle. He prevented any possible controversy over whether he did or didn't cross the invisible line when he scored standing up. Then he fell into the soft white cushion.

Patton kicked the extra point. That made the score—Eagles 7, Cardinals 0, and determined the outcome of the game. Chicago had the ball for only five plays in the final quarter. In the closing minutes Ernie Steele intercepted a pass by Cardinal Pat Harder to quash Chicago's last hope.

As the clock ran out, the Eagles were knocking at the touchdown door again. They had the ball on the Chicago two-yard line when the gun brought play to an end.

In spite of the close score, the game was a one-sided contest, in terms of yardage gained by rushing. The Eagles led in that department—225 to 96. Ground gained by passing was negligible on both sides.

Philadelphia Eagles vs. Chicago Cardinals

Steve Van Buren, Eagle star, was the leading ground gainer, with 98 yards. He was also the hero of the contest by virtue of scoring the game's lone touchdown. Once he exploded for 26 yards—a long gain indeed for a game such as this one had been. Quarterback Tommy Thompson had run the team magnificently, faking effectively and handling the ball well at all times in spite of the snow and cold.

It was Frank Kilroy's recovery of that Cardinal fumble, however, that set up the last-quarter situation for Van Buren's snowy heroics. Steve never disputed that.

Steve Van Buren (15) dives across the Cards' goal line for the only touchdown of the game.

4

Cleveland Browns vs.
Los Angeles Rams
At Cleveland
December 24, 1950

It was the day before Christmas, 1950. The Cleveland Browns and the Rams of Los Angeles were scheduled to meet in what was widely expected to be one of the most momentous battles in the history of professional football. Unlike many such predictions, the game turned out to be just as tremendous as the experts had forecast.

There were two outstanding quarterbacks playing in this match that would decide the championship of the National Football League. The Browns, leaders of the Eastern Conference, had Otto Graham, often called an "aerial wizard" by the sports writers. The Rams, on top in the League's Western division, had California's native son, Bob Waterfield, who was rated as another of the great pros.

Waterfield got his team off to a head start in the first half-minute of play. He did it with a 30-yard pass to Glenn Davis, the former Army speedster.

Bob Waterfield

Cleveland Browns vs. Los Angeles Rams

Davis caught the ball just short of midfield, then ran 52 yards to score, turning the pass into an 82-yard touchdown. Waterfield kicked the extra point, and the Rams had a quick 7–0 lead.

Half a dozen plays later, the Browns evened the score with Graham's 31-yard touchdown pass to Dub Jones. Lou Groza's conversion kick sailed over the crossbar, to make a 7–7 tie.

Otto Graham

Then the Rams, in possession again, put on an eight-play scoring drive. Dick Hoerner capped it by smashing across the goal line from the 3-yard line. Again Waterfield kicked the point, making the score —Rams 14, Browns 7.

Early in the second quarter, Otto Graham went to work again with his specialty. The result was a 35-yard touchdown pass to Dante Lavelli. Once more Groza came in to try for the extra point. The pass from center was not good, however. Without time to place the ball accurately for a precision placement kick, Tom James jumped up and tried to pass for the point. The attempt failed. There was no further scoring in the quarter, so the Rams led at half-time, 14–13.

The missed point did not appear too important in the third period when Graham again passed to Lavelli for another touchdown. This one covered 39 yards, and when Groza kicked successfully for the extra point, the Browns enjoyed a 20–14 edge.

Then the Rams dealt the Browns two quick blows. Waterfield threw three straight completions to put Los Angeles on the Cleveland 1-yard line. From there Dick Hoerner crashed over for his second touchdown. The conversion by Waterfield put the Rams back in front, 21–20.

Right after the ensuing kickoff, Marion Motley,

Cleveland Browns vs. Los Angeles Rams

Cleveland's star ball carrier, fumbled on the Browns' 6-yard line. Larry Brink, Ram end, grabbed the ball and ran it over for a stunning six-pointer. Waterfield's kick gave his team a 28–20 lead.

The two Ram touchdowns came within a space of only 21 seconds. They gave the Los Angeles team an eight-point margin at the end of the third period. Things looked dark for the Browns.

But Graham still had some ammunition left. Before the last quarter was five minutes old he uncorked his fourth touchdown pass. Rex Bum-

Rex Bumgardner (90) reaches for Graham's fourth touchdown pass of the afternoon.

gardner caught the ball in the end zone. Again Groza's kick was good, but because the Browns had not made the extra point following their second touchdown they still trailed—by one point, 28–27.

The two teams battled back and forth indecisively. After two punt exchanges, there were five minutes left to play. The Cleveland fans were worried and fearful. Then the Browns' Tommy Thompson intercepted a Waterfield pass at midfield. Graham, taking over again, hit Dub Jones with a 22-yard pass. The fans went wild.

Taking the Rams by surprise, Graham himself carried on a run that took him to the Los Angeles 21. There, however, he fumbled and Milan Lazevich recovered the ball for the Rams. All seemed lost for Cleveland, and gloom settled over the stands.

The Rams could not make first-down yardage and Waterfield got off a long punt. Cliff Lewis received on the Browns' 14 and returned the ball to the 32.

The Browns were in possession, but they were 68 yards from the Rams' goal line and only one minute and forty-eight seconds of playing time remained.

Graham tried to pass but could find no receiver clear. He ran the ball himself, making 14 yards and going out of bounds. This stopped the clock.

On the next play, Graham passed 15 yards to

Bumgardner in the left flat. Bumgardner ran out of bounds and again the clock was stopped.

After missing on another pass, Graham was successful with one to Jones in the right flat. It was good for a first down on the Rams' 22.

Alternating coolly, Graham again hit Bumgardner with a toss in the left flat. Bumgardner caught the ball and stepped out of bounds on the 11.

Looking at the clock, Graham saw there were 40 seconds to go. On a "keeper" play, he sneaked the ball for only a 1-yard advance, moving it laterally for better field position.

Then he turned toward the Cleveland bench and waved. Every one of his teammates was doing the same thing—waving and calling "Groza!"

It was only second down—but Graham decided to rely on Groza's kicking ability rather than gamble with a pass.

The clock showed 28 seconds left. James crouched for the snap from center. Back came the ball. Groza's head was down, his foot swinging. His toe connected, and the ball sailed over the crossbar, almost dead center between the two uprights—a perfect 16-yarder.

With the scoreboard showing Cleveland 30, Los Angeles 28, the frantic crowd paid scant attention to the 20 seconds of play remaining. After the

kickoff, a 55-yard Ram desperation pass was intercepted by Warren Lahr for the Browns. The gun sounded; the game was over and the season was ended.

The game performance of the two teams had been as close as the score. The Rams outrushed the Browns, 95 yards to 73, and outpassed them, in terms of yardage gained, 312 to 298. The Browns, however, completed 22 passes out of 33 attempts, to the Rams' 18 out of 32. The Cleveland team also intercepted five enemy forward passes while the Rams made only one interception.

Lou Groza, then in his fifth year of pro football, has gone on—and on—to score more points than any other player in pro history. His 43-yard field goal in the 1964 playoff game against the Colts broke a scoreless tie in the second half and pointed the Browns toward an upset victory.

No matter how many more points he goes on to score, though, the chances are that those three he kicked to beat the Rams in the closing seconds of that 1950 game will shine brighter than all the others.

Bears and Rams both watch as Lou Groza's winning field goal sails between the uprights, giving Cleveland the 1950 championship.

5

Los Angeles Rams vs. Cleveland Browns At Los Angeles

December 23, 1951

The year 1951 was a historic one for sports
enthusiasts. For the first time, a fan on the East
Coast did not have to rely on the radio, or on the
next day's newspaper, to follow a major sports event
on the West Coast, or vice versa. Television finally
had linked the two regions visually. The 1951 NFL
play-off was the first ever to be telecast nationally,
and the game was one worthy of the occasion.

The Cleveland Browns, defending champions,
had won the All-America Conference crown four

times in a row. Then they had moved into the
National Football League and had won the championship there, too. For five successive times they
had been title holders.

On the other hand, the Rams had not won a title
since 1945. That was the year the club left its
original Cleveland location and transferred to the
sunnier climes of California, to become the Los
Angeles Rams. Twice they had fought their way
into the play-off. But in 1949 the Philadelphia
Eagles had shut them out; and in 1950, just a year
earlier, the Rams had dropped a heartbreaker to
Cleveland, by just two points in the last half-minute
of play.

Now the Rams were getting another shot at the
seemingly invincible Browns. The weather for the
play-off at Cleveland the year before had been
atrocious. But this time the day was ideal, and the
playing surface was perfect.

All season Joe Stydahar, the Rams' head coach,
had been alternating his quarterbacks. He would
use Bob Waterfield as a starter in one game and
Norm Van Brocklin in the next. He also alternated
the two men by periods. Waterfield was the starter
today. For the Browns, passing-genius Otto Graham
was at quarterback.

No one scored in the first period. In the second,

Los Angeles Rams vs. Cleveland Browns

however, the Rams made a touchdown to culminate a 55-yard drive. Dick Hoerner, their 220-pound fullback, bulled across from the Cleveland 1-yard line. The successful conversion made the score Rams 7, Browns 0.

Fullback Dick Hoerner lands on his back in the Cleveland end zone for the first score of the 1951 championship game.

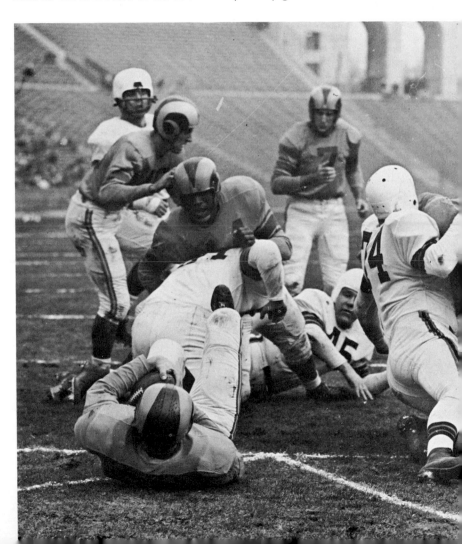

Then came a record-setting field goal by Cleveland's Lou Groza. He made it after the Browns' counter-drive had stalled at midfield. Groza's great kick carried 52 yards and sailed across the bar to make the score—Rams 7, Browns 3. It was the longest field goal in play-off history, and in 1964 still held the record.

A few minutes later, Cleveland again struck quickly. Graham connected for three straight passes. The last one, to Dub Jones, was good for 17 yards and a touchdown. That and the extra point gave the Browns a 10–7 lead at intermission.

The third quarter was a half-dozen minutes old, with the Browns in possession. Graham dropped back to pass. The Rams' Larry Brink, all 240 pounds of him, stormed past the Cleveland quarterback's protectors and hit Graham hard. The impact made Graham fumble the ball and Ram Andy Robustelli grabbed it. Running with it, he got clear to the one-yard line before Cleveland tacklers brought him down.

"Deacon" Dan Towler then made three straight thrusts at the Browns' line. On the third one, he smashed across for a Ram touchdown. The kicked extra point put the Rams back into the lead, 14–10. That was the score when the third period ended.

In the fourth quarter Marv Johnson, a Los

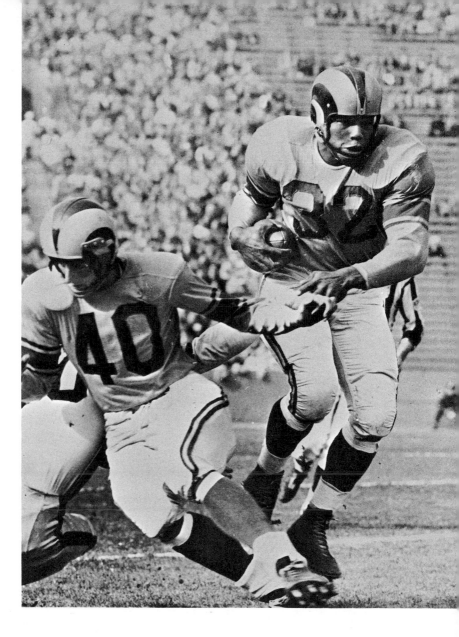

Rams end Elroy Hirsch blocks for "Deacon" Dan Towler (32),
as he goes for 10 yards against the Browns.

Angeles defensive back, intercepted one of Graham's aerials. It led to another Ram score on a kick by Bob Waterfield. The talented quarterback's 17-yard field goal extended the Los Angeles lead to 17–10.

The Browns, however, responded with a spirited 70-yard drive during which Graham personally picked up 34 yards with a sprint down one sideline. Ken Carpenter, Cleveland back, carried the ball over for six points from the 1-yard line, and Groza's kick tied the score at 17–all.

The Browns kicked off and the Rams put the ball into play on their own 20-yard line. Norm Van Brocklin, now quarterbacking for the West Coast team, dropped back to pass. He wanted to throw to Tommy Fears, a Ram end. Fears had started down one side, then cut across. He gathered in Van Brocklin's accurately thrown pass while speeding between defenders Tom James and Cliff Lewis.

Fears, a former college gridiron hero at U.C.L.A., was big and strong. He was also very shifty but not particularly fast. As the two Cleveland defenders took after him, everyone in the stadium thought they would certainly bring him down from behind.

By outrunning his pursuers to complete a 73-yard touchdown play, Tom Fears became the hero of the 1951 championship.

Like everyone else, Fears knew his pursuers were speedier than he. But he had a burning desire that gave him an edge on them. They gained on him— but not enough to bring him down. He crossed the goal line untouched to complete the 73-yard play. It was only the third pass he had caught that day. Waterfield came into the game to kick the extra point and make the score 24–17.

Neither side managed to score again, although there were almost eight minutes more of playing time. The Rams had needed three or four breaks to win, and they had gotten them.

Groza, who had kicked the longest field goal in play-off history, had also missed an earlier try for one from less than half that distance. A Cleveland touchdown pass, from Graham to MacSpeedie, had been called back because of a holding penalty against the Browns. Rookie Andy Robustelli, after recovering Graham's fumble in the third quarter, had carried the ball 34 yards, juggling it all the way as he tried to get a firm grip on it. Finally, Van Brocklin had thrown that perfect pass to Fears, and the Ram end had outraced two faster opponents to score the winning touchdown.

In the years that followed, the Rams were to make it to the play-off only once more. That time they lost. But on this amazing day in 1951 Los Angeles fans saw their favorites win the championship with one of the greatest passing plays ever seen anywhere.

6

Detroit Lions vs. Cleveland Browns At Detroit

December 27, 1953

Jim Doran was a big, gangling Iowan who had
been signed as an end by the Detroit Lions after his
graduation from Iowa State in 1951. He never
achieved all-star prominence, but he continued to
play for the Lions for almost a decade. The Lions
used Doran mainly as a replacement for such
established stars as Leon Hart and Cloyce Box.
When the gigantic Hart hurt his knee in the first
half of the 1953 play-off game, Doran came in to
take his place.

The Big Play

That year, 1953, was the second straight one in which Detroit led the Western Conference and contended in the play-off for the NFL championship. In 1952's big game, the Lions had won over the Cleveland Browns to assume the pro-football crown. Now, as defending champions, they again were playing the Browns, who had succeeded themselves as leaders of the Eastern Conference.

Under the skillful quarterbacking of Bobby Layne, and with heavy reliance on the ball-carrying and kicking of their great back, Doak Walker, the

Doak Walker carries the ball.

Lions had trounced all their 1953 opponents, with the exception of the Los Angeles Rams. The Rams, who had beaten Detroit twice, nevertheless remained a couple of games behind the Lions in the final standings.

The Browns had chalked up an even better record than the Lions during the regular campaign. In fact they were unbeaten right up to the last game of the season, when they suffered an upset defeat at the hands of the Philadelphia Eagles. The Browns' quarterback, Otto Graham, again had been the outstanding passer in the Eastern division. He had executed more completions than anyone else in the league.

The Browns were sure, then, to be a formidable foe; but the Lions were keen to make their record two in a row over the star-laden Clevelanders. The Detroit team also had another strong incentive for winning: This was the first time the Lions would be appearing before a home crowd in a play-off game since the mid-1930s.

The Browns, three-point favorites to win, suffered a bad break at the start of the game. They had received the kickoff and were in possession on their own 24. Otto Graham, the Cleveland quarterback, tried to get off a pass on second down. Lion defender Joe Schmidt got to him and hit his arm before he could get the ball away. Graham fumbled and Les Bingham recovered for Detroit on the 13-yard line.

The Lions scored in six plays, with Doak Walker going across to score the touchdown from the one. When Walker also converted, the Lions led, 7–0.

The Browns continued to have a bad half until finally a Detroit fumble gave them the ball on the Lions' six-yard line. Even then the Cleveland team could not move the pigskin over their foes' goal line on the ground. Lou Groza came in to kick a field goal from the 14, to make the score 7–3. (He was to score two more field goals before the final gun.)

Late in the second period, the Lions' Jim David intercepted a Graham pass and returned it 35 yards to the Cleveland 20. Then a Detroit touchdown pass that would have extended the Lions' lead was called back because an ineligible receiver had caught the ball. Two plays later, Walker kicked a field goal from the 22-yard line to give the Detroiters a 10–3 margin.

That was the score at the end of the half. So far, the game had been relatively unexciting. Sloppy play, fumbles and collisions between teammates had marred the action. A desperation bid by the Browns for a field goal in the last few seconds, with Groza kicking from 51 yards away, had missed.

In the third period, Gorgal intercepted one of Bobby Layne's passes to give the Browns possession. Then Cleveland put on a sustained drive for a touchdown, going 51 yards in eight plays. Jagade scored on a 9-yard plunge. Groza kicked the extra point to tie the score at 10–10.

The game went into the final quarter with the teams all even. The Browns got another break when Colo, their left tackle, recovered a fumble by the Lions' Bobby Layne. After they had driven to the 7-yard line and found themselves stalled there, however, Groza kicked a 15-yard field goal. Now Cleveland led, 13–10.

When the Lions got the ball, Layne went to the air once more. Two good passes and some effective ground plays brought Detroit to the Browns' 26, but there the drive floundered. The Lions tried for a field goal but the kick was not good. The home-team fans groaned, fearing that this had been the Lions' last chance.

They were to get further reason for pessimism. In seven plays the Browns went from their own 20-yard line to the Lions' 35. Again the Detroit defense stiffened, and again the Browns called on Lou Groza. The big fellow's kick was a good one; it covered 43 yards—the longest successful boot of the day. This gave Cleveland a 16–10 margin, with less than five minutes to play.

Then Layne started an aerial bombardment from the Detroit 20. Three completed passes and two plunges brought the ball to the Browns' 33. Two of Layne's tosses went to Jim Doran, now in at end for the injured Leon Hart. One of them was a fine 18-yarder. On it, Doran fooled the Cleveland back who was covering him, by using some fancy footwork that put the Detroit end in front of the de-

Jim Doran hauls in the pass which gave Detroit the 1953 championship.

fender to make the catch.

With 33 yards to go, Layne again faded back to pass. Doran broke for the end zone. This time it seemed as if Warren Lahr, the Cleveland defender, had him well covered. Somehow Doran managed to get behind him.

Layne's throw covered more than 40 yards. It was a perfect strike and Doran grabbed it in the end zone as the crowd roared in a frenzy of appreciation.

The touchdown made the score 16–16. The clock showed two minutes, eight seconds left when Doak Walker kicked the extra point that put the Lions ahead, 17–16. The Detroit fans erupted in jubilation.

The Browns' desperate last-ditch effort was to no avail. A pass interception gave the Lions possession and they held it till the time ran out.

Jim Doran had waited a long time to make his first touchdown reception of the 1953 season. He couldn't have picked a better time to do it. During his near-decade of play for the Lions he snared the modest total of 19 touchdown passes. That one post-season catch in 1953, though, put his name right up there with those of such Detroit luminaries as Bobby Layne, Doak Walker, Yale Lary and other Lion greats of the 1950s.

7

Detroit Lions vs.
Baltimore Colts
At Detroit
October 20, 1957

In 1956 the Detroit Lions had finished second in
the NFL's Western Conference race; they were
runners-up to the Chicago Bears. In their first 1957
game the Lions were soundly beaten by the Baltimore Colts, 34–14, in Baltimore. Then the Detroiters scored two victories and seemed to be
straightened out. Their schedule now called for a
second shot at the Colts, this one in Detroit's Briggs
Stadium before a packed house. The Lions would
have to reverse their earlier defeat by Baltimore if

they expected to stay in contention for leadership of the Western Conference.

They were facing a strong rival, one on the way up. After having been doormats in the Western Conference for years, the Colts had become a strong team. For one thing, they had acquired Johnny Unitas, the brilliant passer who was to go on to become a great star. The Lions would have to contain Unitas and mount a strong attack of their own to win this crucial game.

They gave little indication of doing either in the first half. In the opening quarter the Colts marched to a touchdown, going 68 yards in 14 plays. Unitas passed to Jim Mutscheller for the touchdown, and Bert Rechichar kicked the extra point. The score was Colts 7, Lions 0.

In the second period Jim Martin booted a 47-yard field goal for the Lions, to make the score 7–3. Unitas, however, kept flinging those passes and twice more he hit for touchdowns. The first went to Lenny Moore, the play covering 72 yards. The second, to Mutscheller, was another long one, with Mutscheller going 52 yards after taking the toss while running full stride.

The Lions did manage to get to the Colts' 21-yard line, where they lost the ball on downs. It was not an impressive effort, and the score was 21–3 against

Detroit at half-time.

Before the third period was four minutes old, Unitas completed his fourth touchdown pass of the afternoon. He pegged it to Lenny Moore, in the end zone. When the Colts failed to convert, the score was Baltimore 27, Detroit 3.

Tobin Rote had replaced Bobby Layne at quarterback for the Lions in the second quarter. Layne was a big, strong, fearless player who had been an All-America choice while at the University of Texas. He had been a great performer as a pro, too, but in this game he seemed to be off his form. The crowd had expressed its disapproval loudly before Rote replaced him.

In the third quarter Rote passed over the middle to Steve Junker for a Lion touchdown. The extra point for the successful kick brought the Detroit score up to just 10—against Baltimore's 27. The Lions' cause appeared virtually hopeless.

In the last period, Layne came back in at quarterback for Detroit. The crowd booed him again, but he quieted them in a hurry. Three passes— one to Hopalong Cassady, one to Junker and another to Cassady—were good for a touchdown. Layne kicked the extra point, making the score— Colts 27, Lions 17.

There were eight minutes left to play. The fans

Tobin Rote, former Green Bay quarterback, hurled a touchdown pass for the Lions during the third quarter.

began to believe that the Lions still had a chance.

Their hopes got a bad jolt the next time Detroit had possession. The Lions were in good position for a drive from midfield, but Baltimore's rookie back, Andy Nelson, intercepted a pass that Layne was aiming at Dorne Dibble. Now the Colts had the ball at midfield.

But luck was not favoring the Colts either. On their second play after recovering, Alan Ameche fumbled and Jim David got the ball back for the Lions. In three plays, it had changed hands twice.

After two incomplete passes, Layne threw one that Cassady grabbed on the Colts' 32-yard line. There were two minutes left.

John Henry Johnson made a first down around left end. Layne uncorked a 30-yard aerial to Cassady, who was brought down on the 1-yard line. Johnson smashed over left tackle to score, and the extra point made the score—Colts 27, Lions 24.

There was only a minute and a half left to play. The Lions needed a break now, desperately.

They got it. After the Colts received the kickoff, they lost yardage on two running plays. Moore tried to circle left end. It was a standard play—a sweeping run that, if successful, would make a first down; if not, the Colts could punt on fourth down.

Moore fumbled when he was close to the sideline. The ball hit on its forward point and bounced back onto the playing field. If it had bounced from its hind point it would have cleared the sideline and the Colts would have retained possession for a punt from their own 29-yard line.

As it happened, a Lion pounced on it in fair territory for a Detroit recovery. Less than a minute

Hopalong Cassady (40) about to snare a pass for the Lions.

remained. The crowd roared a frantic plea for a miracle.

Layne called on his favorite receiver of the day, Cassady. Hopalong was in the end zone, waiting, when Layne's throw reached the spot. The kicked extra point made the score Lions 31, Colts 27. With Detroit ahead for the first time in the game, the scoreboard clock showed 46 seconds left to play.

The Colts had more than half a minute to retaliate, and half a minute could be plenty for Johnny Unitas. He made one successful throw. On his second attempt, most of the Detroit secondary swarmed through to blitz him. He fumbled and Detroit recovered. The Lions ran one play before the gun ended one of the greatest games ever seen in Detroit.

In this, his final season with Detroit, Layne was to lead the Lions through a Western Conference play-off and to the NFL championship. There was plenty of hair-raising action during the rest of the year. But none of the subsequent thrills matched those of the day when Lenny Moore's fumble bounced the wrong way for the Colts and the right way for the Lions.

8

San Francisco Forty-Niners vs. Detroit Lions At San Francisco

November 3, 1957

At the end of the 1964 season, the great passing star, Y. A. Tittle, announced his retirement from the ranks of the active professionals. He had played for 17 years in the National Football League—a distinguished career during which he set many records.

The marks he set will shine in the record books for quite a while—most touchdown passes, lifetime; most touchdown passes in one season; greatest passing yardage, lifetime.

In spite of all these records, "Yat" considered

that his greatest football thrill was one in which he participated only as a sideline observer. It occurred during the New York Giants' final game of the 1961 season, which ended in a tie with the Browns and clinched the Eastern Conference lead for the Giants. As the scoreboard clock ticked off the last seconds, a crowd of 60,000 roared them out in a tumultuous gridiron countdown: *"Ten . . . nine . . . eight . . . seven . . . six . . ."*

Tittle, on the bench, jumped up to shout the numbers along with everyone else.

Tittle's own biggest play was made for another team, in a different place. In 1957 he was playing for the San Francisco Forty-Niners, on a team that came closer to making the NFL play-off than any other Forty-Niner eleven. The place was San Francisco's Kezar Stadium.

The previous year, 1956, the Forty-Niners had staggered through a losing season. They had won five, lost six and tied one. In 1957 they started off as though they weren't going to do much better, losing to a supposedly weaker team, the Chicago Cardinals, 20–10. The following week, while they were preparing to face the Los Angeles Rams, the Forty-Niners were far from light-hearted. They did not relish the prospect of another losing season.

Tittle, as he later recalled the scene, was as grim-faced as any of them.

Practice scrimmage was dragging to an end. His receivers were failing to get into position. Defensive linemen were all over him. Assignments were being missed time after time. Dropping back to pass and seeing he was about to be trapped again with no receiver in the clear, Tittle flung the ball straight up into the blue, disgusted.

The ball rose in a high arc and started down in the vicinity of offensive end R. C. Owens, who was surrounded by a number of defensive backs. Owens was a former basketball player who had enjoyed considerable success as a hoop man at the University of Idaho. Later he had put his phenomenal jumping ability to good use playing for the famed Harlem Globetrotters.

When Owens saw Tittle's wild throw coming his way, he reacted as if he were grabbing a basketball rebound. He leaped straight up in the air and came down with the ball—only this time it was a football, not a basketball.

Everyone stared at him, open-mouthed. From the sideline, someone yelled, "That's our 'Alley Oop' play!"

From then on, the "Alley Oop" was a vital part of the Forty-Niners' offense. The expression is one

Covered by two Lions, Forty-Niner R. C. Owens reaches for one of Tittle's famous Alley Oop passes.

adapted from that of circus performers on the trapeze or high wire who call out, *"Allez!"* (the French word for "Go!") as a traditional take-off signal.

As developed by the Forty-Niners from its accidental beginning, the "Alley Oop" was simply a high, arching pass—as high as Tittle could throw it—in the general direction of the opponents' goal line. Its success depended on Owens' kangaroo type of jumping prowess. All he had to do was to jump higher than the defenders gathered around him. They knew what he was going to do, but generally they were helpless to prevent it.

The Sunday after the Alley Oop was born on the practice field, Tittle and Owens used it to beat the Los Angeles Rams in Kezar Stadium. The following week Owens helped beat the Chicago Bears with a catch he made in the end zone while on his knees; but a week later he gathered in an Alley Oop from Tittle for a victory over Green Bay. The next game was another winning effort against the Bears.

Then came the great game against the Detroit Lions in Kezar Stadium. It was an exciting, seesaw struggle. The Forty-Niners trailed by 10-0 in the second quarter, but enjoyed a slim 14-10 margin at intermission. In the third quarter they scored another touchdown to increase their lead over the Lions to 21-10; and in the fourth they added still another to raise it to 28-10.

At this point the Lions' quarterback, Tobin Rote, took things in hand. He threw three straight touchdown passes, with Bobby Layne kicking the extra point each time. The last one, made with only one minute and 20 seconds to play, put the fired-up Lions out in front, 31–28.

With San Francisco in possession after the kick-off, the correct Ram strategy was obvious: short passes and a determined effort to conserve time by stopping the clock as often as possible. Everyone in the stadium, including the Lions, knew it.

Tittle threw three short passes in a row. All three were completed, and on two of them his receivers managed to squirm out of bounds to stop the clock.

Then came another pass, with the receiver again stepping out of bounds. Following that, Hugh McElhenny carried the ball in a run that ended as he stepped past the sideline. Now the Forty-Niners had the ball on the Lions' 41-yard line, with 19 seconds left on the clock.

There was one play possible, and only one. The Lions dropped everyone back into the secondary defense zone except for a four-man line up front.

With the snap of the ball these four put on such an aggressive rush that Tittle had to scramble to elude them. He was at midfield when he threw a cloud-grazer. As he let the ball go, the onrushing Lions hit him hard. He watched the rest of the play sitting down.

R. C. Owens had raced to the one-yard line. There he came to a dead stop, to be joined by

Detroit players Jim David, Jack Christiansen and Carl Karilivacz. They outnumbered Owens three to one, but the tense fans were counting on the amazing springs in those legs of his.

The ball was coming down. Owens braced for the leap. So did the three Lions. Four pairs of hands reached high for that ball, but it was Owens who grabbed it—and held it.

He tumbled into the end zone. The six points scored on the spectacular play put the Forty-Niners ahead, 34–31. The extra point, which made their total 35, was icing on the cake.

Two months later the Forty-Niners knew bitter disappointment when they lost the Western Conference play-off to these same Lions. After that, the Alley Oop went the way of so many trick plays that blossom for a while, then fade.

But that one play which scored the winning points for his team with only 11 seconds left in the game must rate as the greatest that Y. A. Tittle ever made. It outshone all his other 2,117 regular-season completions.

9

New York Giants vs. Cleveland Browns At New York

December 14, 1958

The Cleveland Browns had been having one of their typically strong seasons. They appeared to be well on the way to repeating their 1957 performance, when they were first in the Eastern Conference. Jimmy Brown, the great fullback, then in his second year with the Cleveland team, was en route to a new mark for individual rushing yardage for a single season. With only two weeks remaining in the season, it looked as if the Browns were sure to win another Conference title.

The New York Giants had been waging a valiant uphill struggle to catch the Browns in the standings. Their position looked fairly hopeless until, with a little luck, they eked out a two-point victory over the tough Detroit Lions.

So the Eastern Conference race was still alive when the Browns came to New York to face the Giants on December 14, 1958. A victory, or even a tie, for the Browns would make it impossible for the Giants to catch up. But if the New Yorkers won, the Conference outcome would not be decided for another week. A tie, however, would do the Giants no good. If they got only a tie, they would be sunk.

So the Giants had their backs to the wall on this shivery-cold Sunday. Still, they knew the Browns could be beaten. They had done it themselves earlier in the season—and in the Cleveland park. Today the Giants were playing at home. They were grateful for whatever slight advantage that might give them. Certainly the great majority of the 63,000 fans jamming the stands would be giving them strong vocal support.

Warming up on the sideline, Pat Summerall, the Giants' big place kicker, felt his injured right foot with cautious fingers. Jim Lee Howell, the New York coach, watched Pat questioningly. Then he looked at Don Chandler, the Giant punter, who

Giant place kicker Pat Summerall displays one of his special kicking shoes.

had also had some place-kicking experience. He motioned Chandler to warm up.

However, Summerall kept on testing his foot, hoping he wasn't just imagining that it was beginning to lose the stiffness that had hampered him. He was a veteran of half a dozen campaigns in the NFL but this was his first season with the Giants.

A light snow was falling when the game started. It tended to obscure the action, and in the first minute of play it seemed as if New York's hopes might be vanishing with the snowfall, too.

The initial play from scrimmage, with Cleveland in possession, was a faked handoff. Jimmy Brown wound up with the ball, and was off like a cannonball. Not bothering with deception, he rocketed up the middle. Giant players bounced off him like so many tennis balls, and he rumbled across the goal line at the end of a 65-yard run.

Many of the fans, still getting settled in their places, missed that first score. People all over the stands were asking, "What happened?" The six points went up on the board before the game was a minute old. The kick was good and added a seventh.

The Giants, playing with dogged determination, managed to keep the Browns from another touchdown in the first half. Although Lou Groza kicked

Breaking loose from his Giant tacklers, Jimmy Brown scores a touchdown in the first minute of play.

a field goal for the Clevelanders, the Giants matched it with one of their own. The New Yorkers were encouraged by the fact that Summerall, having indicated he was ready, went in to do the kicking on the play. With Charlie Conerly holding, he confidently swung his right foot and booted the ball in a soaring arc between the uprights.

When the half ended with the score 10–3 against them, the New Yorkers still felt some optimism as the result of Summerall's successful field-goal kick. They also had noticed something during the action that might help them later.

On one play, Conerly, the Giant quarterback, had handed off to Frank Gifford, who had then tried a halfback pass to Alex Webster, the fullback. Gifford, who had been nursing a sore elbow for three weeks, failed to get the proper stuff on his throw and it missed Webster. However, when Kyle Rote, the other running back, returned to the huddle he reported that he had spotted a flaw in the Browns' defense that might help the Giants later.

When Gifford had swung off on the attempted pass, Rote had noticed that the Cleveland secondary defenders had moved too far to that side—had overshifted. Conerly tucked the information away in the back of his mind.

In the second half, the Giants were charging better on defense, and they were bottling up the explosive Jimmy Brown effectively. But they couldn't seem to carry out a sustained offensive of their own. It began to look as if they would not get a chance to try the play suggested by the alert Rote's earlier observation.

Then Andy Robustelli recovered a Cleveland fumble on the Browns' 45-yard line. It was New York's opportunity and Conerly was ready to make the most of it.

On the play, Conerly sent Gifford swinging wide. As expected, the Browns' defensive backs moved over with him. After feinting a block at the Cleveland tackle on the other side of the line, Rote swung away and tore down the sideline.

Braking to a sudden halt, Gifford threw a long, high pass diagonally across the field. Through the falling snow it arched—and Rote caught it. He reached the 6-yard line before a tackler brought him down.

Two plays later, Conerly decided to try it again. This time Gifford, using the same maneuver, hit Bob Schnelker in the end zone. The extra point was kicked to tie the score, 10–10.

As far as the Browns were concerned a tie was all they needed. If they could keep New York from scoring again they would leave the Stadium with the Eastern Conference leadership clinched. They wouldn't have to tally again themselves.

The Browns' strategy was clear: They must keep possession of the ball, and send running plays into the line in an effort to run out the remaining time.

But the Giants were fired up now. They put on a tremendous defense, jamming up the middle of the line, stopping the Cleveland runners in their tracks.

Twice the Browns were forced to punt. One of

the kicks was a poor one and the ball went skittering out of bounds after covering only a short distance. The Giants had a chance for a field-goal shot from the Cleveland 31. Summerall made the try, and his kick went wide.

The fans were silent. They didn't think the team would get another chance.

Then the Giants fought their way a dozen yards into Brown territory. There were two minutes left. A field-goal attempt from here would have to be made almost from midfield.

First Jim Lee Howell thought he would have Conerly try a pass to get in a little closer. Then he changed his mind. The wind was blowing, and Conerly had already missed with three attempts. One had covered 55 yards, only to slip through Webster's hands on the goal line.

Summerall trotted out from the bench. The crowd emitted a great roar. He had already succeeded with one kick, missed with another. The one he missed had been from 20 yards less than the distance would be now.

Carefully Conerly brushed away snow to make a bare spot for the ball. Summerall was telling himself to keep his ankle "locked." Sometimes he forgot and let it flex. This was no time to forget.

The ball came back. Quickly but with great care

Pat Summerall (right) boots the ball high and true for a field goal.

Conerly placed it down. The blockers did their job well. Summerall's kick sailed high and true. It carried 20 yards past the cross bar. Over-all it was a 70-yard boot.

It scored three points for New York, won the ball game for them, 13–10, and forced a play-off to decide the Eastern Conference championship. The Giants won the play-off, too, and faced the Colts in the NFL title game. But that was another story.

This one had been decided by the big three-point play that featured Pat Summerall's not completely healthy kicking foot.

10

Baltimore Colts vs. New York Giants At New York

December 28, 1958

More than 60,000 fans were crowded into Yankee Stadium, shivering a little on this misty late-December afternoon. It was the third Sunday in a row that the New York Giants had come to the Stadium to display their gridiron power and finesse. Twice they had met and defeated the Cleveland Browns. The first time they had boosted themselves into a tie for the leadership of the NFL's Eastern Conference; the second time they had knocked Cleveland out of the Conference title that had earlier seemed a sure thing.

Now the Giants were ready once more to perform before a Stadium audience, but this time they were facing the Baltimore Colts, winners of the Western Conference title. The Giants had beaten them in an earlier game, one played during the regular season.

The fans were savoring the prospect of exciting action to stem from a notable quarterback rivalry. On one side was Charlie Conerly, the graying veteran who directed the New Yorkers' offense. On the other was the Colts' young, crew-cut Johnny Unitas, who three seasons before had been playing sandlot football in Pittsburgh.

Jim Lee Howell, who had coached the Giants to their first League championship two years earlier, was at the helm of the New York club. The rival coach was Baltimore's Weeb Ewbank, a chunky little man wearing a brown suit he considered lucky.

Ewbank was relying on something more than luck, though. He had a great deal of confidence in the ability of young Johnny Unitas, who then was on the threshold of one of the great careers in professional football.

In 1955 Johnny had been playing with a semi-pro team from Pittsburgh. His NFL home-town team, the Steelers, had signed him out of the University of Louisville but before the season began they cut him from the squad to make room for a more highly regarded player. Unitas telephoned Paul Brown, the Cleveland head coach. But Brown had just succeeded in persuading his veteran star quarterback, Otto Graham, to come back for one more season.

At the end of the year, however, the Baltimore Colts' front-office boss, remembering Johnny's name, invited him to attend a Colt tryout camp. Once there, Johnny soon made a place for himself on the Baltimore roster. Now, after only two years of NFL experience, he was leading the Colts in their race for the biggest football prize of all, against a team that was used to the pressure of play-off games.

Johnny Unitas (19) gains 16 yards for the Colts in a game against the Giants.

In the first half, the trend of the game indicated that the surprising Colts were headed for an easy victory. The Giants drew first blood, however. Conerly's pass to Frank Gifford was good for an eye-opening 40 yards. Pat Summerall followed that up with a 36-yard field goal. The score was—Giants 3, Colts 0.

In the second quarter, Big Daddy Lipscomb recovered for the Colts as the Giants fumbled the ball on their own 20-yard line. The Baltimore quarterback sent Lenny Moore and Alan Ameche alternately skirting the outside and spearing up the middle. Then Ameche plunged across for the Colts' first touchdown; the kicked extra point made the score—Colts 7, Giants 3.

Before the period was over, Baltimore staged a much longer march. Starting from their own 14-yard line, the Colt ball carriers battered away at the Giant line—five and six yards at a clip. They drove past midfield, into Giant territory. Here Unitas switched to the air, completing two tosses to Ray Berry. The second one was good for 15 yards and another touchdown. The conversion kick gave the Colts a 14–3 lead.

Coming into the second half with that 11-point lead, the Colts seemed bent on increasing their margin. They drove down the field until the Giants made a formidable goal-line stand on their own 3-yard line.

Then it was the New Yorkers' turn to thrill their supporters. Up to this point, Conerly had been using Kyle Rote to receive short passes. Now he sent Rote down the left sideline, to cut sharply to the right. Rote took Conerly's pass near midfield and lugged it right to the Baltimore 25-yard line. There two Colts tackled him, and he fumbled.

As the ball dribbled away from Rote, players on both sides stood for a split-second, frozen. Then Alex "Big Red" Webster, the heavy-duty Giant back, grabbed the pigskin and carried it to the 1-yard line. From there Mel Triplett crashed over for six points. A successful kick followed to make the score—Colts 14, Giants 10.

Now the run of the action began to favor the Giants. Their great defensive linemen, Andy Robustelli and Dick Modzelewski, were getting through to harry Unitas in the passing pocket.

The New Yorkers took possession and Conerly came up with a new target for his passes, Giant end Bob Schnelker. First he hit Schnelker with one good for 17 yards. Then he came right back with another that covered 46 yards and turned the stands into pandemonium. The ball was on the Baltimore 15.

Baltimore Colts vs. New York Giants

On the sideline the Giants' strategists were
huddled around the bench looking at a Polaroid
print. Wellington Mara, their talent director, had
dropped it from his lookout atop the Stadium. It
showed that the Colts' secondary pass defenders
were shifting over too far whenever a New York
offensive play indicated strength to the right side.

Coach Jim Lee Howell sent in directions for a
pass play that would have receiver Frank Gifford
go out wide to the left while the main thrust seemed
aimed at the right. Conerly and Gifford executed
the play flawlessly. It went for a touchdown which,
with the point-after, put the Giants ahead, 17–14.

There were only two minutes left before the final
gun. Unitas and the Colts went to work. They had
the ball on their own 14. Their strategy was simple
and obvious. Unitas had to connect with Ray Berry,
his best receiver, enough times to score.

Three times he tried. Three times he succeeded,
even though the Giants were double-teaming Berry
and had a pair of defenders on him each time. The
second of Berry's three catches was accomplished
with a spectacular flying leap.

His third reception put the ball on the Giants'

Charley Conerly (42) gets off a long pass to Kyle Rote, while
Gino Marchetti tries vainly to stop the play.

13-yard line. The New Yorkers looked shaken.
With the clock running out, the Colts frantically
waved for the field-goal kicking team. Steve Myhra,
former Notre Dame guard, took his stance to wait
for the ball to be out in position. Myhra had succeeded in making less than half of his field-goal
tries that season, and in this game a first-period
effort of his had been blocked by the Giants' Sam
Huff.

The ball was put down 20 yards from the uprights. Myhra swung his foot and as the ball went
over the crossbar the thousands of Baltimore fans
in the stands went wild. With seven seconds left,
the scoreboard towering over the bleachers pro-
claimed the tally—Baltimore 17, New York 17.

When the final gun sounded, seven seconds later,
the situation called for the first overtime in a quarter
of a century of football play-offs. After play resumed, the first team to score would be the winner.

After the three-minute intermission, a coin was
flipped. The Giants won the call and chose to
receive.

On the first Giant play from scrimmage Gifford
carried for a four-yard gain. Then Conerly tried a
pass to Schnelker that failed. After another incom-

Raymond Berry, Unitas' best receiver, leaps for a pass.

93

plete forward, it was fourth down and six to go. Unwilling to punt and give the Colts possession, Conerly called another pass play but all his receivers were covered too closely.

Desperately the veteran quarterback ran with the ball himself, trying to go around right end. Bill Pellington, the Colt linebacker there, hit him but Charlie kept on going. Don Shinnick, another defender, rammed into the struggling pair in a way that finally stopped Conerly's forward momentum.

The officials had to call for the sideline markers for a measurement. It showed that Conerly had been stopped just a foot short of making a first down. The ball went over to the Colts.

Two Baltimore plays netted a five-yard loss. With third down and 15 to go, Ray Berry caught a pass from Unitas that was good for a first down. Then Ameche on a trap play drove through the middle for 23 yards.

Three more yardage-gainers followed. One of them was a dangerous pass from Unitas to Jim Mutscheller out in the right flat. Had a Giant defender intercepted it, he could have gone all the way for a winning score. But that didn't happen: Mutscheller snared the pass and the play ended with the ball resting on the Giants' 1-yard line.

A power play was the obvious thing. Unitas

called it—Ameche carrying, to go outside tackle.

The big Baltimore back got the blocking he needed. He smashed over for the six points that won the game.

The final score in the first overtime contest in NFL play-off history was—Colts 23, Giants 17. What many regard as the greatest pro-football contest ever played was won by a combination of Johnny Unitas' brilliant passing, Ray Berry's inspired receiving and Alan Ameche's awesome running.

Alan Ameche lies buried under an avalanche of Giant defensemen after smashing through for the winning Colt touchdown.

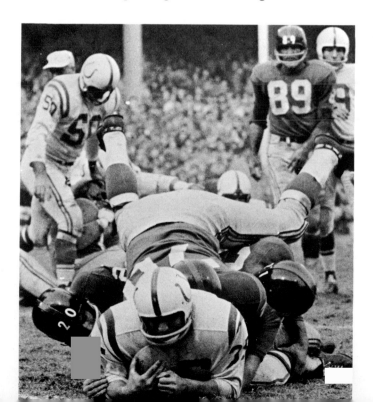

11

Philadelphia Eagles vs. New York Giants At New York

November 20, 1960

The rivalry between the Philadelphia Eagles and the New York Giants has been one of the most intense in the National Football League. It goes back more than three decades. The New Yorkers' team physician, Dr. Francis Sweeny, once remarked:

"Every time we play those guys, we have to bring at least one of our players home through the window."

The doctor was referring to the fact that when

an injured man is on a stretcher, he cannot be taken off the train through the door. It isn't possible to make the necessary turn. The solution is to open a window in the coach. Through that, half a dozen husky football players can pass their injured teammate without upsetting the stretcher. The husky Giants were frequently unloading a battered teammate through a train window after a rough game with Philadelphia.

In November of 1960 the Eagles were apparently en route to their first championship since those captured by the great teams coached by Greasy Neale in 1948 and 1949. Between 1949 and 1960, no Philadelphia team had been able to win more than seven games in a season.

Buck Shaw had taken over as Eagle coach in 1958. Under him the team had bettered its performance, winning more than it lost in 1959. By the 1960 season, his players were keenly aware that they had a good chance to become champions again.

The season started badly for the Philadelphians when the Cleveland Browns handed them a 41–24 trouncing. But after that, the Eagles clicked off six straight victories. They were leading the Eastern Conference of the NFL when they got ready to play two successive games with the Giants. The

Tommy McDonald (25) gets clear to receive a pass from Norm Van Brocklin (11) during an Eagle–Packer game. This passing combination put the Eagles back in the race for the first time in ten years.

first was being played in Yankee Stadium; the second was scheduled for Philadelphia.

Eagle quarterback Norm Van Brocklin, obtained from the Los Angeles Rams in a trade, had developed into a first-rate signal caller. Clearly he was on the way to his best year as a professional player. And flankerback Tommy McDonald was snaring touchdown passes in game after game. Chuck Bednarik was amazing his teammates and the whole sports world: at the ripe old football age of

35 he was playing on both offense and defense. Besides filling the offensive-center spot he was the middle linebacker on defense. And he played the whole game, without relief. No one has attempted such a double role since.

Truly, Bednarik was one of Philadelphia's all-time stars. Quaker City fans had watched him play four years with the University of Pennsylvania and in 1960 he was in his twelfth year with the Eagles. Chuck knew virtually every blade of grass on Franklin Field.

On November 20, 1960, however, Chuck and his teammates were forced to battle the fired-up Giants at Yankee Stadium. And the New Yorkers refused to concede an inch to their favored opponent. The Giants assumed command from the opening kickoff. In the first period, Joe Morrison's one-yard touchdown plunge followed a perfect 50–yard pass from George Shaw to Kyle Rote. Pat Summerall's conversion gave the Giants a 7–0 lead.

They extended their margin to 10–0 in the second quarter. Pat Summerall scored the three points when he booted a 26-yard field goal.

This was the score at half-time: Giants 10, Eagles 0. It looked as if New York were going to hand Philadelphia a walloping. The Eagles had gained only 31 yards rushing during the first 30 minutes

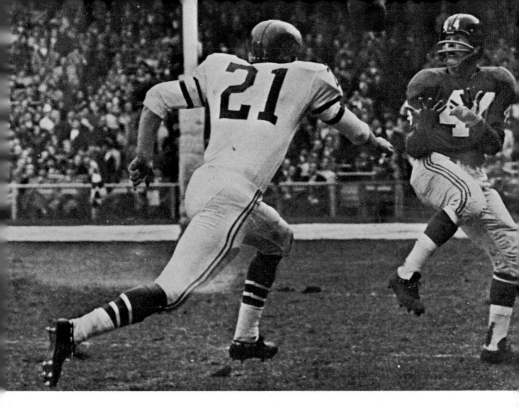

Kyle Rote (44) catches a 50-yard pass from George Shaw during the first quarter. The Eagles' Jim Carr (21) is too late to intercept.

of play. Van Brocklin had been able to complete only one forward pass.

Almost nine minutes of the third quarter were gone before the Eagles managed to post their first score. They did it when Van Brocklin flung a touchdown pass to McDonald. The play covered 35 yards. Bobby Walston kicked the extra point to make the score—Giants 10, Eagles 7.

Philadelphia, still struggling to catch up, continued to trail until the last five minutes of the final quarter. Then Walston booted a 12-yard field goal that brought the score to 10–10.

With the Eagles kicking off, Ed Sutton made a fine return for the Giants. Shaw, who was substituting at quarterback for the injured Charlie Conerly, was doing a good job for the New Yorkers. Then, on the Giants' own 38-yard line, a handoff from Shaw to Mel Triplett, New York's fullback, was messed up.

Unable to gain full manual control of the ball, Triplett juggled it as he ran. Chuck Bednarik hit him hard, jarring the ball completely out of Triplett's grasp. Eagle line-backer Jim Carr caught it in midair and nobody could overhaul him as he ran for a long touchdown. Walston made the extra point; the Eagles led, 17–10.

With only two and a half minutes left in the game, the Giants fought desperately to catch up, unleashing a violent passing attack. Frank Gifford received a pass that gave the New Yorkers a first down on the Eagle 49.

Two plays later Shaw pegged a long one. Bob Schnelker, who had raced under the crossbar of the Eagles' goal posts, reached for it—only to see it slide off his fingertips. Schnelker pounded a goal post in frustration. The fans groaned.

The next play Shaw called was a pass to Gifford.

The Eagle secondaries swarmed in on the snap of the ball, red-dogging Shaw. However, he managed to get the pass off to Gifford, who caught the ball on the 30-yard line.

Don Burroughs stopped Gifford with a low tackle. At the same instant, Bednarik came in from the other side, charging high. When the big Eagle defender hit Gifford, the crunch seemed to resound all over the stadium. Gifford went down, the back of his helmeted head hitting the turf with terrific impact. The ball squirted out of his limp hands, and

Bednarik (60) charges into Gifford (16), knocking him out of the game.

Chuck Weber recovered it for the Eagles.

Bednarik got to his feet. Gifford was still stretched on the ground, arms spread, face up. When the Eagle linebacker saw his opponent helpless and his own team in possession of the ball he raised his arms high in exultation.

It was a purely unthinking reaction on Bednarik's part. But when the throng in the stands saw it they started booing. To them it looked as if he were enjoying Gifford's misfortune.

Then Bednarik, aware that Gifford was seriously injured, crouched solicitously over the fallen Giant. He rose and stood quietly while Gifford was placed on a stretcher and carried from the field.

The game ended with the score 17–10 in favor of the Eagles. Their fine late rally, plus the two untimely fumbles by the opposition, accounted for the Philadelphia triumph.

On both the fumbles, it was Bednarik's awesome tackling that made a Giant player lose the ball. Vince Lombardi, coach of the Green Bay Packers, has said, "The name of the game is blocking and tackling." Bednarik's play bore it out on this November, 1960, day.

Gifford was hospitalized and he played no more that year. He also remained inactive for the whole 1961 season. When he came back to help the Giants win the Eastern Conference title in 1962 and again in 1963, he played as a flanker. His days of heavy contact had been finished by that one smashing contact with Bednarik.

For a while Bednarik had a hard time living down the villain role the New York fans pinned on him. There was no ill will or malice in Bednarik, however. He simply played the game the only way he knew how—for all he was worth.

Jim Lee Howell, then the New Yorkers' head coach, took some of the pressure off the Eagles' linebacker when he said, "There was nothing wrong with the way Bednarik tackled Frank. There's only one way to tackle in this league—as hard as you can. And Bednarik did it that way."

Chuck Bednarik, one of the Eagles' all-time greats.

12

Green Bay Packers vs. Baltimore Colts At Green Bay

October 8, 1961

Paul Hornung, Green Bay's star ball carrier and kicker, struck for a Packer touchdown in the first two minutes of play. The 38,000 fans crammed into Green Bay Stadium to see the Packers play the Baltimore Colts appreciated it but they did not get especially excited. After all, Hornung had struck early in other games. The previous year he had amassed a total of 176 points for an all-time single-season professional record.

Following the extra point—kicked by Hornung

—the first period saw no further scoring. The crowd settled back to watch what they expected would be a tough, tight ball game. The Colts had lost their former leadership of the Western Conference, the Packers having taken it over the previous year. But Baltimore still had most of the players who had brought it world championships in 1958 and 1959.

No one could expect to run roughshod over Baltimore's Johnny Unitas and Company. That first explosive 54-yard run of Hornung's, coming so early in the game, had probably caught the Colts a bit off balance. It was doubtful if it would happen again.

Looking like the Colts of old, the Baltimore team began to grind out the yardage late in the period. Starting from their own 28-yard line, they went all the way to score. Lennie Moore plunged across the goal on the second quarter's second play. The good conversion kick tied the score, 7–7.

In the next sequence of plays, the Packers reached the Baltimore 31-yard line. A roughing-the-passer penalty against the Colts helped them get there. At this point Bart Starr, the Green Bay quarterback, missed on three consecutive passes. Hornung stepped back and kicked a 38-yard field goal. The Packers led again, 10–7.

Following the kickoff, the Colts put the ball in play in their own territory. Then Jesse Whittenton intercepted a Unitas pass to give the Packers possession on Baltimore's 37. Battling a stubborn Colt defense, Green Bay pushed its way down to the enemy 1-yard line. Starr's passing and fullback Jim Taylor's rushing were the main weapons.

Then, from the 1-yard line, Hornung smashed over the goal line with a thrust outside tackle. Again he booted the extra point. Now the score was 17–7 and the crowd cheerd its favorite long and loudly.

The count stayed at 17–7 at half-time. It didn't remain there long after play was resumed. On the third play of the third period, Dave Hanner, the gigantic Packer lineman from Arkansas, grabbed off one of Unitas' passes. He intercepted on the Baltimore nine, and advanced a yard before he was hauled down.

Hornung carried but made no gain. Then Starr hit him with a pass in the end zone. It turned into Hornung's third touchdown, and he quickly added his third good extra-point kick to put the Packers out front, 24–7.

Still the blond halfback from Notre Dame wasn't finished. Green Bay's Willie Wood put his teammates on the scoring trail again with another pass interception. He snagged Unitas' toss deep in

Baltimore's back yard. Starr connected with passes
to Max McGee and Ron Kramer that ate up yardage. The one to Kramer put the Packers on the
Colts' 10-yard line.

There the ball went to Hornung again. And once
more Hornung smashed across for a touchdown—
this time on one play. After his fourth touchdown
he kicked his fourth extra point. The score was 31–7
and no end seemed in sight.

Although the touchdown was the last for Hornung, it wasn't the last for Green Bay. Willie Wood
took a Baltimore punt on the Packers' 28, and with
good blocking went all the way. His 72-yard beauty,

Charging through the Colt defense, Jim Taylor gains yardage for Green Bay.

with Hornung's following good kick, made the score—Green Bay 38, Baltimore 7.

In the final quarter, the harassed Unitas fumbled the ball near his own goal line and the Packers recovered. They quickly crossed the six-point line, with Jim Taylor carrying it over on a three-yard plunge. Hornung added the extra point to make the score 45–7.

After that the Packer second-stringers came out on the field for a fling in the sunshiny afternoon. The teams battled through the final ten minutes with no further score.

The Packers followed up this game with a great

Paul Hornung (5) dives into the end zone to score his fourth touchdown of the day.

season. They repeated as the leader of the Western Conference and then went on to win the NFL championship. Hornung did not match his point total of the previous year, but his performance against the Colts put his name in the NFL record book. His 33 points scored in a single game has been topped only by Ernie Nevers' 40 against the Bears in 1929 and Dub Jones' 36, also against the Bears, in 1951.

The Packers intercepted six Colt passes in their

smashing win. Willie Wood had shone with his brilliant punt runback, Bart Starr with his passing and Jim Taylor with his jolting rushes. But the performances of all of them were dimmed by Hornung's tremendous overall play. When he took that first handoff from Starr and circled left end for his 54-yard jaunt into the end zone, it was the dramatic overture to a bravura performance.

Three reasons for Green Bay's success: (left to right) Bart Starr, Jim Taylor, Paul Hornung.

13

Washington Redskins vs.
Cleveland Browns
At Cleveland

September 23, 1962

Bobby Mitchell was back in town—back in the
city on the shores of Lake Erie where he had started
as a rookie with the Cleveland Browns five years
earlier. Now, though, he was in Cleveland as a
member of an underdog Washington team, the
Redskins. The Cleveland Browns had traded him
away after the 1961 season.

The deal had sent Mitchell, Cleveland's best ball
carrier (except for the great Jimmy Brown), and
Leroy Jackson to Washington. In return, Cleveland

had acquired the Redskins' draft right to Ernie Davis, the 1961 Heisman Trophy winner and number one college football prospect.

There were several reasons why Bobby Mitchell wanted to turn in a top performance on this particular afternoon. The one he declared publicly was the fact that so many of his friends who lived in the Cleveland area would be watching or listening to the game. He didn't mention his feelings about having been traded from a team that regularly was in the thick of the fight for the NFL championship to one that had won a total of only nine games during the four years he had been in the league.

Washington's head coach, Bill McPeak, had switched the swift Mitchell from his accustomed spot as running back to the flanker's position. During the Redskins' opening game of the season, this change had paid off handsomely. In sparking the team to a 35–35 tie with Dallas, Mitchell had scored three touchdowns and lost a fourth one when the play was nullified by a foul call. Besides returning a kickoff 92 yards, Bobby had tallied on an 81-yard pass play, with Norm Snead doing the throwing.

In spite of the success of the Snead–Mitchell combination, the experts had picked the Browns as strong favorites to win this game. They predicted

Bobby Mitchell (left) and Norm Snead—the hope of the Redskins.

that the Cleveland team would drub the Redskins by 16 points. They were relying on the fact that the Browns had held the underdog Redskins to a total of only five touchdowns in the last four league games played between the two teams.

Mitchell would have to do some really remarkable playing to help the Redskins break their nine-game losing streak against the Browns. The jinx went way back to a 30–30 tie in 1957.

Washington managed to zoom ahead early in the game, however. The Redskins' safety man, Jim Steffen, intercepted a Cleveland pass and returned it 39 yards for a touchdown. Bob Khayat booted for the conversion and the Redskins led, 7–0.

Lou Groza, the Browns' field-goal specialist and all-time field-goal-kicking master of the NFL, then made a field goal from 32 yards out, to make the score 7–3. This was the first of six field-goal attempts by the Cleveland ace.

In the second period, Cleveland's Tom Wilson plunged for a one-yard touchdown, which with the extra point put the Browns into the lead, 10–7. Later in the quarter, the Redskins got into Cleveland territory. When their attack sputtered out, Bob Khayat tried a 40-yard field goal but his kick was short.

Then, following a pass interception by Cleveland, Groza booted a three-pointer from the 12-yard line. This gave the Browns a six-point margin, at 13–7. Before the half ended, the Cleveland attack got going once more, then stalled on the Redskins' 23. Groza's toe went into action again, but this time the great kicker's boot went wide to the left.

The miss didn't seem too serious, however—especially when Khayat attempted another field goal for Washington in the last minute of the half and again fell short with his kick.

Between the halves, the Redskins' coach stressed to his players that they were trailing by only half a dozen points. McPeak pleaded with his men to settle down and play their game—their running game. The coach wanted his team to move on the ground, to take advantage of Cleveland's concen-

118

tration of defense against the pass threat posed by Mitchell.

"Use Mitchell as a decoy," he urged Snead, his towering quarterback. "If they zone Bobby they'll weaken themselves somewhere."

Determined to carry out McPeak's plan, the Redskins trooped out onto the field for the second half. The only score in the third period came when their Bob Khayat kicked a 33-yard field goal.

Now Washington was only three points behind. But in the fourth quarter, Groza brought the Redskins' point deficit back to six when he booted one over the bar for Cleveland from the 37-yard line. It made the score 16–10.

Mitchell returned the ensuing kickoff from the Redskins' nine-yard line to their 38. Then the Washington team drove into Brown territory before bogging down. A ten-yard loss was followed by an incomplete pass. Then the Browns intercepted a Redskin toss on the Cleveland 34.

With only five minutes of playing time left, Washington's hopes were beginning to fade. But the Redskins got a break when Jimmy Brown fumbled a swing pass at midfield and Eddie Khayat, second member of Washington's brother act, recovered the ball for his team.

Taking over on the Redskins' 33-yard line, Snead

ran five straight running plays. The ball was resting on the midfield stripe. With two minutes left, Washington called for a time-out.

McPeak, motioning his quarterback over to the sideline, said to Snead, "Now we pass."

On the next play, Snead threw to Mitchell for only the second time in the period. Bobby had dropped back from his flanker spot and taken a halfback position.

Snead barked the signals, took the center pass and dropped back. Mitchell, cutting across, was partially blocked by Brown linebacker Galen Fiss. He broke free, spun across the middle and took a short bullet pass from Snead.

Gathering in the ball, Mitchell pivoted and started off at an angle. With his great speed, he drew away from the two Brown defenders on his side of the field. No one was near him when he hit the end zone. He roared across the line like a runaway sports car.

The clock showed one minute, thirty-six seconds left. The score was 16–16. Dick James held the ball for Bob Khayat to try the conversion. The ball went between the uprights to put the Redskins one point ahead.

Then the Browns put on a frenzied drive. Throwing short passes, Jim Ninowski completed four out of five to take his team from its own 27-yard line to the Washington 28. Seven seconds of playing time were left when Lou Groza stepped back to try a 34-yard field goal.

Whipped into a frenzy of their own, the Redskins poured through. At least two of them got in the way of the ball to block the kick.

But the game wasn't over yet. The Browns' Bobby Franklin managed to fling himself on the bouncing ball. The Browns still were in possession, now on the Washington 43.

Two seconds were left—time for one play. Again Groza stepped back, this time to the 50-yard line.

The ball was snapped. This time the Cleveland line fended off the charging Redskins—except for one man.

Rod Breedlove, Washington's right linebacker, came rocketing through. The kicked ball hit him. Half a dozen players were chasing the skittering pigskin when the final gun banged.

Bobby Mitchell got his wish, but not until the last minutes of a hard-fought game. When Snead and he combined to make that 50-yard touchdown, the result was one of the big upsets of the 1962 season, as well as one of the outstanding plays in Redskin football annals.

14

Dallas Cowboys vs.
Philadelphia Eagles
At Dallas

October 14, 1962

All the morning of that memorable 14th of October, 1962, rain had fallen, and it still was drizzling at game time. The bad weather, plus the fact that the Cowboys had not managed to win a single home game since September of the year before, made the Texas fans stay away in large numbers. Only about one-quarter of the seats in Dallas' double-decked Cotton Bowl were occupied.

Those who did rally to the support of the home team on that wet afternoon, however, were to be rewarded with a couple of historic plays. They also watched the Cowboys run up their highest score since NFL football had come to the Southwest in 1960.

The last time the Cowboys and the Eagles had met, Philadelphia had given Dallas a thorough walloping. One of the Eagles feared most by Dallas was pass-catching star Tommy McDonald. In his college days, McDonald had been an outstanding player at Oklahoma and was therefore well known to Texas football crowds. If Tommy had one of his big afternoons, he might well sink the Cowboys, almost by himself.

The Dallas player assigned to the unenvied job of covering McDonald was a rookie replacement, Mike Gaechter. The Dallas club had signed Gaechter mainly on the strength of the speed he had demonstrated as a sprinter at the University of Oregon.

A season earlier, the Dallas team had acquired another collegiate speed-merchant from the Pacific Northwest. Like Mike Gaechter, Amos Marsh was a sprinter, but he had attended Oregon State. During his freshman year with Dallas, Marsh had scored one touchdown.

The Cowboys got off to a slow start, failing to score in the first period. Bobby Walston, the

124

Eagles' kicking ace, booted a pair of field goals to give his team a six-point lead. The first one was made from 36 yards out. The second came after a fumble by the Cowboys' Don Perkins, which was recovered by Philadelphia player Don Burroughs on the Dallas 25-yard line. Five plays took the ball to the Dallas 2-yard line. When the Cowboys' defense stiffened there, Walston kicked his second three-pointer from the 9.

The Cowboys moved into the lead in the second period. The first score for Dallas came on a field goal kicked by Sam Baker. Then Amos Marsh put the Cowboys ahead with a touchdown. He made it on a 20-yard smash through the middle, after having skirted left end for the same distance. Just before the half-time intermission, little Eddie Le-Baron, who was sharing the Dallas quarterbacking assignment with Don Meredith, flipped an 8-yard pass to Frank Clarke in the Eagles' end zone. The Cowboys trotted off the field with a 17–6 lead.

In the third period, Clarke caught another touchdown pass, thrown by Meredith this time. The Cowboys were ahead, 24–6—and the stage was set for the dramatic final period.

Baker started it with a field goal on the opening play of the quarter, boosting the Cowboys' lead to 21 points. Then the Eagles struck back. King Hill, who had replaced Sonny Jurgensen as the Philadelphia quarterback, threw a 26-yard pass to McDonald. It was ruled complete on interference by Gaechter, and subsequently Hill scored on a 1-yard quarterback sneak. Now the tally was 27–12.

Walston kicked off for the Eagles. The ball came sailing into the end zone. Amos Marsh caught it one yard behind the goal line. He took off up the middle, made one cut to his right at the Cowboys' 30-yard stripe, then turned on the speed and was gone. He scored standing up, having covered the length of the field and a yard to boot. It was the first 100-yard play the Dallas team had ever registered.

The Cowboys' 34–12 edge should have seemed a discouraging margin for their opponents at this stage of the game, but the Eagles were in a fighting mood. With King Hill directing the show, they went 70 yards in a dozen plays and scored. Theron Sapp climaxed the drive with a five-yard plunge through the middle of the Dallas line.

Striving to protect their reduced but still comfortable margin, the Cowboys did not have much luck after receiving the kickoff. Attempting to pass from a spread formation, Meredith fumbled. He recovered the ball, but the 9-yard loss forced Dallas to kick. The Eagles took possession about 10 yards inside their own territory.

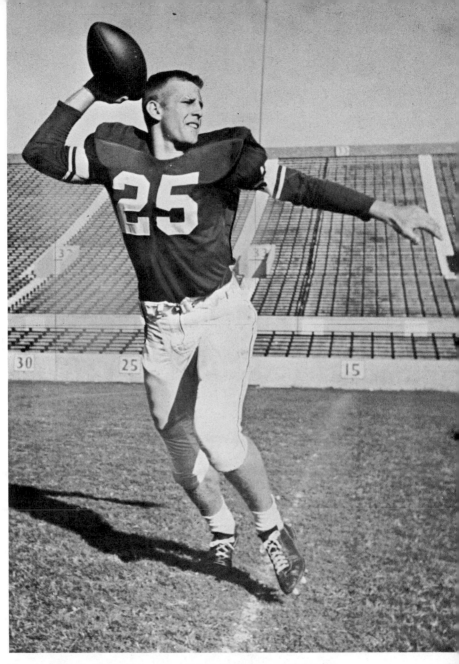

Tommy McDonald had been an outstanding player at Oklahoma.

King Hill, the Eagles' quarterback.

King Hill proceeded to rip off three successive passes. The third one, a 9-yarder caught by Tommy McDonald, put the Eagles on the Dallas 15. Hill tried to hit McDonald again, this time with a peg into the end zone. But there Mike Gaechter stepped into the picture with a startling interception.

Having grabbed the ball, the Cowboys' defensive back shot down the left sideline. No one laid a hand on him until he reached the Eagles' 45. There King Hill and John Wittenborn, a Philadelphia guard, each had a shot at him but the speedster shook them both off and went all the way to score. In his goal-line-to-goal-line trip, Gaechter displayed the fleetness he had shown as a member of the Oregon 440-relay team when they equaled the world record.

The Cowboys never had made a 100-yard play until this game. And now they had given their screaming fans two of them within nine minutes! Any play that covers 100 yards—from one goal line to the other—is a rarity. Two in one game is incomparably more rare. And this pair was extra-special because both were made by the defense, with pure speed being the main factor in each.

The bright stars of the Cowboys' smashing 41–19 victory were, of course, Gaechter and Marsh. However, it was also a highly satisfactory day for Eddie

Dallas Cowboys vs. Philadelphia Eagles

LeBaron, the smallest quarterback in the NFL. He had been tossing passes in the league for a decade, but this was the first time he had enjoyed a perfect afternoon—seven attempts and seven completions!

Eddie LeBaron, the Cowboys' quarterback.

15

Green Bay Packers vs. New York Giants At New York

December 30, 1962

Sports fans sometimes joke about Green Bay, calling it the icebox of pro football. It's just a few miles down the road from the North Pole, according to them.

On the last Sunday of 1962, however, New York City wasn't taking a back seat to any place when it came to cold weather. The thermometer stood at a mere 17 degrees above zero, and the wind was whipping away at 40 miles an hour. Hot coffee froze only a few minutes after it was poured.

The weather had taken everyone by surprise. The evening before had been wet but mild, so anyone who had gone to bed before midnight received a real shock upon awakening. By mid-morning the temperature had fallen to the low 20's. The sun was shining brightly but the wind was piercing.

Such were the weather conditions for the 30th National Football League championship game. The Green Bay Packers, winners of the Western Conference title, were seeking a second straight victory over New York's Giants, leaders of the league's Eastern Division. Yankee Stadium, site of the struggle, was jammed with 62,892 half-frozen but eager fans. The majority of them were vociferous supporters of Coach Allie Sherman's Giants.

The Giants had taken a 37–0 thumping from the Packers in Green Bay a year earlier. But they had been confident they could turn the tables on the Midwesterners this time. They were counting on Y. A. Tittle's passing to more than offset the Packers' formidable running attack and stout defense. Now, with this wind, they weren't so sure.

The Giants didn't intend to let the invaders from Wisconsin walk off with another championship without a fight, though. Come what might, Green Bay would know it had been in a football game!

The New Yorkers planned to zero in on Jim Taylor, the tough Packer fullback. Taylor had scored 19 touchdowns by rushing, during the regular season, and had led the league in both scoring and rushing.

Taylor was indeed a tough gridiron character, but the Packers would need every bit of that toughness for their afternoon's work—plus whatever help an assortment of fine players could offer.

One of the stars Green Bay could count on was Jerry Kramer, their all-pro guard that year. Midway in the first period, Kramer kicked the first of three field goals he would contribute in the game. The Packers settled for the three-pointer after their drive bogged down on the Giants' 19-yard line, having run into a Giant defensive stone wall at that point. The score was—Green Bay 3, New York 0.

In the second period luck seemed to be favoring the defending champions. Phil King, the Giant fullback, fumbled the ball on a rushing play and Ray Nitschke, the Packer middle linebacker, recovered on the New York 28. Paul Hornung's halfback pass to Boyd Dowler took Green Bay to the 7. On the next play Taylor, who seemed almost to be tiptoeing over the frozen turf, went across for a touchdown. When Kramer kicked the extra point, the Packers led, 10–0.

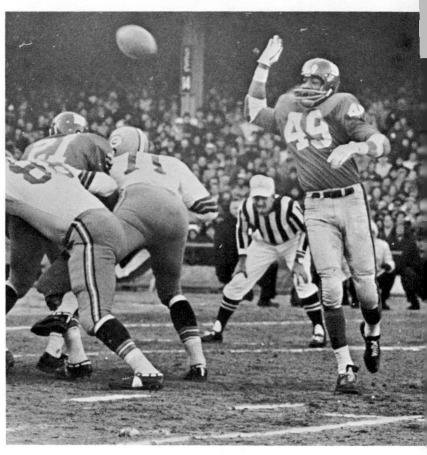

All-pro guard Jerry Kramer (64) kicks a field goal to add three points to the Packers' score.

The Giants had been fooled on the touchdown play. "Reading" it incorrectly, they had shifted their defensive strength to the left side of the line. At the last split-second, Taylor shifted direction and

moved through the middle with no defender laying
more than a few fingers on him.

The first half ended with the score still 10–0. In
the third period, Erich Barnes, the Giants' slick
defensive back, blocked a punt by Packer Max

McGee on the Green Bay 15-yard line. Jim Collier, used only on squads specializing in such chores as running back punts and defending against place kicks, fell on the ball as it bounded into the end zone to score a touchdown for the Giants. By this action, Collier got his name written into the permanent records. Chandler's subsequent conversion kick cut Green Bay's lead to 10–7.

Following the ensuing kickoff, the Packers lost three yards on three plays, and McGee punted. Sam Horner, back to receive it for the Giants, tried to make a shoestring catch on the New York 35 and the ball slipped out of his numbed hands. Ray Nitschke clutched at the free ball and managed to hold onto it. It was Nitschke's second fumble recovery of the game, and the pair of them were enough to bring him honors as the game's most valuable player.

Starting at the Giants' 42-yard line, the Packers fought down to the 22, with Jim Taylor doing most of the gaining. Then two incomplete passes dictated a field-goal attempt. Kramer kicked his number two from the 29-yard line, making the score Green Bay 13, New York 7.

Still another three-pointer was to come from Kramer's talented toe, and it ran the Packers' lead to 16–7. He kicked it from the 30, with two minutes to go in the final period.

For the remaining 120 seconds of the game, the Giants raced the clock as Tittle filled the air with a flurry of passes. But the great quarterback could not cope with the weather and the alert Packer defenders. New York failed to cross the goal line again. The score stood at Green Bay 16, New York 7, at the final gun.

The conditions under which the game was played favored the Packers. The Giants lacked a runner to match the hard-bitten Taylor. Y. A. Tittle's long passes to Del Shofner, ordinarily such a scoring threat, were made inaccurate by the gale that seemed to whirl in several directions at once within the Stadium. The rock-hard turf, which froze as soon as the tarpaulin was taken off, provided scant traction for any kinds of footgear— cleats, sneakers or ripple-soles. The extreme cold made the rigorous body contact on both sides all the more punishing.

It was so cold in Yankee Stadium that the ink in the duplicating machine, used to provide newspaper and radio men with the play-by-play account and statistics, froze during the second period. As a result, the second quarter's play-by-play, the league's official account of the game, can barely be read today. Thanks to quick emergency measures

that were taken, however, the rest of the game play-by-play is clear and readily readable.

In the duplicating machine's story of the second quarter, though, there is a line that seems even dimmer than the rest. It reads: *King fumbled, Nitschke recovered on Giant 28.*

That might almost be the whole story of the 1962 NFL championship game.

Giant Del Shofner is tackled by Wood (24) and Adderley during the 1962 title game.

16

Chicago Bears vs.
Green Bay Packers
At Green Bay

September 15, 1963

"How old is he?" people were saying to anyone who would talk to them about football. "*Sixty-nine! Why, this is a game for young men!* His team's been playing a 1958 offense against a 1962 defense. They're lucky they won as many as they did last year! How can they expect to beat clubs like Green Bay and Detroit?"

They were talking about George Halas and his Chicago Bears. Halas, the founder, owner and coach of the Chicago team, was known popularly as the "Papa Bear." Fans and sports reporters held him in high esteem because of his long record of contribution to professional football. It was widely believed and freely said, however, that the Bears were hopelessly behind the times. Progress had left them in the lurch. They would never catch up with the new concepts. The parade had passed by Papa Bear and he didn't even know it.

Then came the summer of 1963. Stories coming out of the Bears' training camp said the toughest preparation program in Bear history was taking place. The reports didn't make much of an impression, though. An old bear couldn't learn new tricks—so how could he teach them to young bears?

Under the hot Indiana sun, Papa Bear Halas drove himself, as well as his men, unmercifully. Some of the newcomers to the squad were bewildered. No one ever had told them the pros would be like this! The old gent was like a wild man, fuming and shouting all the time. More than one high-priced rookie thought seriously of packing up and going home during the first murderous two weeks.

Halas raged at them, drove them. No one escaped his tongue-lashings. Overweight players were targets for his special wrath, "I'll give you just two weeks," he warned, "to get into shape!"

144

There was no doubt he meant what he said.

The results of this rigorous training schedule had their initial display in the first game of the Bears' pre-season schedule. They were playing the New York Giants at Cornell University's picturesque Schoellkopf Field, high above the waters of Cayuga Lake. The Giants were staying in the Cornell dormitories. The Bears were at Ithaca College. Some of the players on the two teams were hobnobbing before suiting up to get ready for the game.

"Where were you last night?" one of the Giants asked. "We all went to a movie—thought we'd see you downtown."

"Movie?" a Chicago player snorted. "Why, Halas locked us in our rooms after supper! No TV, no radio, no nothing!"

The Bears won the game handily. It looked as if Papa Bear's Spartan program was paying dividends already. At the close of the first half some fisticuffs broke out. Allie Sherman, the Giant coach, watched from his side of the field, expecting Halas and his staff, who were closer, to step in and break up the brawl. Instead, he saw the Papa Bear grab a handy helmet and swing it at the nearest Giant head.

Allie raced across the field and laid a restraining hand on the Chicago coach's arm.

"George," he chided, "Cut it out—this is just a

pre-season game. This isn't for the money!"

As it turned out, every Bear game in 1963 was one for the money. That included the official season opener, against the champion Packers before 45,000 fans in Green Bay.

It was a perfect afternoon. The temperature was in the mid-70's, with bright sunshine and a gentle southerly breeze. The setting seemed exactly right for the Packers to run their string of consecutive victories over the Bears to nine.

The Chicagoans made it quickly apparent, however, that this was to be no walkover for the league champs. Halfway through the opening period, Jim Taylor—Green Bay's all-time greatest rusher—fumbled on the Packers' 33-yard line. Richie Pettibon recovered for Chicago.

The Bears picked up a first down on a pair of carries, by Ron Bull and Rick Casares. Then, after two losses and a short pass, it was fourth down and 13 to go. Bob Jencks stepped in and booted a 32-yard field goal.

Green Bay got the three points back the next time it had the ball. The Packers moved from their own 30-yard line to Chicago's 34. Then, on fourth down and with three to go, Jerry Kramer, Green Bay's durable all-League guard, came back out of the line to kick a 41-yard three-pointer.

146

Chicago Bears vs. Green Bay Packers

In the second period, it began to look like a tough afternoon. After the Bears went all the way from their 34 to the Packers' 2, quarterback Billy Wade fumbled. Green Bay's Henry Jordan recovered but the Packers could not break away from the shadow of their goal posts. They punted out of danger and after an exchange of interceptions the half came to an end. The halftime score was 3–3.

Early in the second half, the Packers fought from their own 20 to midfield. Bart Starr, the Green Bay quarterback, passed to Tom Moore to put the ball

Green Bay's Tom Moore carries the ball into Bear territory.

into Bear territory. Starr tried another pass, only to have Chicago's Roosevelt Taylor step in and pick off the ball.

It was a key play. From their 32-yard line, the Bears rammed 62 yards in ten plays. Joe Marconi

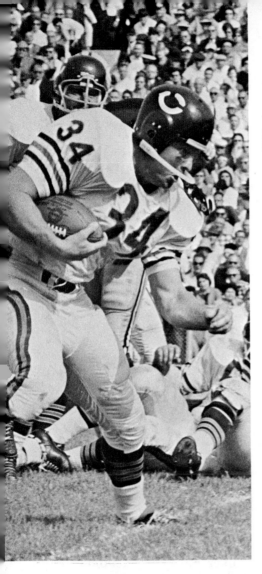

Tearing through the Packer
line, Joe Marconi (34) leads
the Bears to victory.

punctuated the drive when he plunged over the
goal from the 1-yard line. The extra point kicked by
Jencks made the score—Bears 10, Packers 3.

In the fourth period the Bears' third interception
of a Bart Starr pass gave them another chance to

149

A jubilant Coach Halas hugs one of his Bears after winning the 1963 championship.

score. After they reached the Green Bay 20, Jencks tried for a field goal from the 27 but missed.

Close to the end, the Packers were making a last great effort. Veteran linebacker Bill George ruined their hopes when he made the fourth Bear interception on Starr, an unusual experience for the Green Bay hero.

The jubilant Bears had stopped the Packers cold. Their rugged defense yielded only 150 yards to the

Green Bay team—77 of them on the ground. Offensively, they cashed in on the short passing of Billy Wade.

The next day the headlines screamed *Upset!* But the Bears went on to a season that proved it really wasn't. They won their next three games, lost one to the Forty-Niners, and from then on racked up a record marred only by two ties. They won their first Western Conference crown in seven years, and their first League championship in seventeen years.

It all went back to Halas' merciless training program of six months before. Perhaps it wasn't so much a matter of new tricks as of hammering on fundamentals. Whatever the reason, Papa Bear showed everybody he still had what it took in the world of professional football.

17

Pittsburgh Steelers vs.
Dallas Cowboys
At Dallas

December 8, 1963

The season had been a rather wild one for the Pittsburgh Steelers, and it wasn't over yet. First there had been a tie with the Philadelphia Eagles because two extra-point conversion kicks had failed. One had been blocked and the other had hit the goal post. Because there had been two additional ties, and only half a dozen victories, everyone had written the Steelers off as championship contenders.

Yet by December, all that was necessary to make Pittsburgh's final game with the Giants a contest for the Eastern Conference title was for the Steelers to beat the Dallas Cowboys on the afternoon of December 8.

It was a lot easier to talk about this than to do it, however. Dallas, long out of the Eastern race, was completely relaxed. The Cowboys were also determined to make up for the one-touchdown defeat suffered at the hands of the Steelers earlier in the season.

It looked as if this could be a difficult afternoon for the lads from the banks of the Monongahela. When the Cowboys took a quick 9–0 lead, the situation began to look even more difficult. The Dallas team made their score with a 53-yard field goal by Sam Baker, the third longest in National Football League history, and a two-yard keeper play by its lanky quarterback, Don Meredith.

But Steeler toughness is traditional; it began back in the 1930s, when Art Rooney started the Pittsburgh club. It has carried through the days of Dr. Jock Sutherland, Johnny Michelosen and other coaches, right up to the rule of Buddy Parker. Steeler teams have had the reputation of never being out of a game until the final gun sounds. In this game, they had moved back into it by half-time.

Ed Brown, the Pittsburgh quarterback, whose fumble in the first period led to Baker's long field goal, made amends for his misplay in the second period. He threw two long touchdown passes. The first, covering 55 yards, went to Buddy Dial, who made a sensational catch. The second, a 28-yarder, was caught by Preston Carpenter.

With Michaels kicking the extra point after each touchdown, the Steelers went ahead, 14–9. And

The Steelers' left-footed place kicker, Lou Michaels, lets go with a field goal.

before the second period ended, Michaels added a 24-yard field goal to run Pittsburgh's lead to 17–9.

In the third period, Baker kicked another field goal, almost as long as his first, for Dallas. Lou Michaels was short with an attempted field goal for the Steelers. Then Meredith, the Cowboys' quarterback, squirmed to another touchdown by himself; and when Baker converted the Cowboys were in front by two points. They took their 19–17 lead into the final period.

Midway in the fourth quarter, the Steelers fought from their own 20-yard line to the Dallas 46. Quarterback Brown, who was doing the punting for the Pittsburghers, was forced to kick. The ball rolled dead on the Dallas 11. The platoons started their changeover but they were halted by the violent wigwagging of the officials.

The Cowboys had committed a mistake rare in pro football—that of having too many men on the playing field. The ball was brought back to the point where the play had begun, then moved five yards closer to the Cowboy goal line. Lou Michaels came in to try another one of his left-footed specialties but Dallas defensive back Don Bishop blocked the kick.

After three plays with no gain, a Cowboy punt sailed into the Steelers' end zone. There were half a dozen minutes left to play. It was up to the Steelers to make up that two-point deficit or have the season end for them right there.

Ed Brown tried three straight passes. On the first the Cowboy defenders threw him for a loss. He missed with the next two. Now it was fourth down and 14 to go. Brown dropped back to punt; he was standing only a few yards in front of his goal line.

Instead of punting the ball, however, the Steeler quarterback threw a pass to left end Bill "Red" Mack. It was the first pass that Mack, a former Notre Damer, had caught all afternoon. The Cowboys had seen reason to assign more than one man to cover Mack on the chance he might be the receiver on a long-shot pass.

Streaking down the sideline, Mack made a great catch of Brown's surprise toss. He gathered it in at the Pittsburgh 30, then sprinted all the way to the Dallas 42 before a couple of defenders knocked him out of bounds.

Now the Steelers had possession in Dallas territory. Brown decided to use some running plays to work the ball deeper in case it became necessary to try for a field goal. John Henry Johnson went over left tackle for a yard. Theron Sapp picked up 8 yards around right end. On the next play he was stopped for no gain on a smash at right tackle.

157

Steeler Theron Sapp (33) upended by two Dallas Cowboys.

It was fourth down and a yard to go, with the ball on the Dallas 33. If a field goal were attempted it would have to be from about the 40-yard line. Steeler coach Buddy Parker called time out to discuss the problem with Brown.

They decided to go for the one yard necessary to make a first down. Brown gave the ball to John Henry Johnson. The Steeler veteran's unusual claim to fame was that he had scored more points after reaching the age of 30 than any other pro football player in history.

John Henry smashed into right guard. The whole Cowboy team knew he was coming. They stopped him at the knees—but the upper part of John

158

Henry's body had moved forward enough to make the yardage, and the officials signaled a first down for Pittsburgh.

Theron Sapp then took over. He went around left end for seven yards and, on the next play, over right tackle for 23 yards and a six-pointer. The touchdown, followed by Michaels' successful kick, gave the Steelers a 24–19 victory.

As a result, the game with the Giants in New York the following Sunday was the biggest one in the East that season. The Steelers went into it with the prospect of finishing first if they won or fourth if they lost.

They finished fourth. It was that kind of a season for the Pittsburghers. It would be a long time, though, before the Steelers or their fans would forget that exciting gamble that paid off in the final period against the Cowboys.

18

Minnesota Vikings vs.
Green Bay Packers
At Green Bay

October 4, 1964

When pro football came to Minnesota, it was no surprise that the Vikings' natural rivals turned out to be the Packers. Green Bay was only a couple of hundred miles to the east, and it was this amazing Wisconsin town that had helped to form the National Football League back in the early 1920s.

For forty years the Green Bay Packers had enjoyed a monopoly in the loyalty of pro-football fans in the upper Midwest. Now the Minnesota Vikings were on the scene and laying colorful claim to their share of the spotlight.

For three years, however—and twice each season —they had failed to up-end the great teams that Coach Vince Lombardi fashioned in Green Bay. But 1964 might be different. After winning five successive pre-season games, the Vikings had surprised everyone with an opening-day triumph over the Baltimore Colts. True, they had slipped in subsequent games against Chicago and Los Angeles, but they still seemed a team with dangerous potential.

Now they were invading Green Bay once again. The Packers' picture-book stadium, the capacity of which is equal to almost half the population of the city, was crammed as usual. And enough excitement would be crammed into this game for Viking fans to remember a long time. The afternoon's happenings would again demonstrate two truths: *Anything can happen in pro football* and *The game isn't over till the final gun.*

Both teams came into this contest minus the services of their best ball carriers. Tommy Mason, the Vikings' most productive ground-gainer for two years, was out with an injury. Similarly incapacitated was the Packers' great fullback, Jim Taylor.

The Viking coach, Norm Van Brocklin, was relying on Bill Brown and Tom Michel to do the

Minnesota Vikings vs. Green Bay Packers

running chores against the Packers' defense, justly famed as one of the most rock-ribbed in the league. He had to place most of his hopes, though, on the unusual abilities of quarterback Fran Tarkenton, who had been Minnesota's signal caller ever since the team began, in 1961.

Fran Tarkenton

After retiring as a University of Georgia gridiron star and joining the Vikings, Tarkenton had added a special ingredient to professional football. Most pro quarterbacks drop back to pass from what is known as the "pocket." This is an area from which they can operate while being protected by teammates who fend off any opposition players charging through into the offensive squad's backfield. Occasionally the quarterback will take a step or two to either side, seeking a better passing angle. He may move around some to give his potential receivers more time to get into the right position for catching a pass.

Tarkenton, however, has become famous for "scrambling"—running around, zigzagging and evading would-be tacklers by sheer quickness and shiftiness. This type of action carries the risk of his being thrown for a big loss but it also makes possible a big gain when that risk is accepted. A receiver given an extra second or two to break loose can mean a touchdown.

It is impossible to set up an effective defense against a "scramble" pass attack. No one, even the man who is doing the scrambling, knows which way he is going to move, or when.

No one scored in the opening quarter of the

October 4, 1964, game, but the Vikings were on the march. At the end of the period they were on the Green Bay one-yard line. Tarkenton had connected twice with Tom Hall on third-down passes to keep a 67-yard drive going. After play was resumed, Bill Brown dove across the goal line for a touchdown. When Cox kicked the extra point, Minnesota led, 7–0.

Green Bay struck back quickly, scoring on a 50-yard pass from Bart Starr to Boyd Dowler. Paul Hornung's attempt to convert failed when Viking Rip Hawkins blocked his kick. Hornung had failed to get sufficient height into the boot. Now it was Vikings 7, Packers 6.

Again Tarkenton went into action as he hit Hall on third-down pass completions. This time he drove his team 78 yards, with Brown once more smashing over from the 1-yard line. Cox matched his first extra-point kick with another successful one to give the Vikings a 14–6 margin.

Just as quickly, Green Bay countered with another touchdown. Hornung carried the ball across on a short rush after Starr made a series of completions to his favorite receiver, Dowler. This time Hornung's kick was good, to make the score Minnesota 14, Green Bay 13. There it stood at half-time.

The Vikings ran into a bit of bad luck at the start

of the second half. Bill Brown fumbled on the first play from scrimmage and the Packers recovered the ball on the Minnesota 32. Then, with a spectacular over-the-shoulder catch Dowler took a long pass for a touchdown. Hornung's kick was good for a point, and Green Bay went ahead for the first time, 20–14.

Now it was Green Bay's turn for some bad luck. Hornung made a fumble on his team's 19, and Jobko recovered the ball for the Vikings. After several short gains on the ground, Tarkenton passed to Hall for another six-pointer, after having first scrambled all over the field, or so it seemed. The extra point was kicked to put Minnestota back in front, 21–20.

In the fourth quarter, the Packers staged a sustained march from their own 10 to the Vikings' 12. Moore made a couple of fine runs and Starr pitched "strikes" to Kramer and McGee during the drive. On fourth down, Hornung booted a field goal from the 20 to restore the lead to Green Bay, 23–21.

The Vikings received the kickoff, then lost the ball, but managed to get possession again with less than two minutes of playing time left. Tarkenton reached Hall with a pass good for 14 yards. He hit Michel, the rookie halfback, with another that gained 13. On his next try, Michel was held to one yard. Then Tarkenton was thrown for an 8-yard

Green Bay's great quarterback, Bart Starr, gets off a pass.

loss as he failed to get off a pass. When he threw from beyond the scrimmage line on third down, a penalty put Minnesota back five yards.

Now the Vikings faced a fourth-down situation, with 22 yards to go, on their own 36. Less than a minute's playing time remained and they had no time-outs left. This was their last chance.

The Packers were deployed in their "prevent" defense. Tarkenton feared that, if his receivers ran their usual patterns, they would be unable to shake themselves clear far enough down the field to do any good. Without revealing his intention in his team's huddle, he decided he would scramble purposely to allow them to go deep into Packer territory.

Back went the ball. Back went Tarkenton. He ran to his right as Big Willie Davis, Packer end, chased him. Tarkenton reversed and ran left as Davis pursued desperately, trying to get his hands on the Viking quarterback.

Finally Tarkenton spotted Hall, his right halfback, deep—and all alone—on the right sideline. He threw the ball, and then to his alarm saw Gordy Smith, Viking right end, also sprinting toward the air-borne pigskin. Smith did not realize that Hall was the target. He didn't even know Hall was in his path.

Minnesota Vikings vs. Green Bay Packers

When he was just a step away from Hall, Smith clutched the ball, then swerved as his teammate came into his line of vision. He ran it ten yards farther, to the Packer 21.

The clock ticked away remorselessly. Michel hit the left side of the line for two yards, bringing the ball into position for a last-chance try for a field goal. Out onto the field came Fred Cox and the Vikings' field-goal squad.

Cox's toe connected with the leather and over the cross bar sailed the ball, from 27 yards out. With the clock showing 18 seconds remaining, the scoreboard read 24–23, in favor of the Vikings.

That was the way it ended. The Vikings grew up that afternoon, and went on to their first winning season. Tarkenton's great fourth-down pass against staggering yardage may have been the turning point.

The big play—Fred Cox's field goal in the last 18 seconds of play.

19

St. Louis Cardinals vs. Cleveland Browns At St. Louis

December 6, 1964

The Cleveland Browns were in a confident mood.
They had advised the manager of the motel where
they were staying in St. Louis that they would be
needing the big dining room for a victory celebra-
tion after the game with the Cardinals in the afternoon.

A victory at Busch Stadium would clinch the
Eastern Conference crown for Cleveland. Then,
with first place sewed up, their season-finishing
game against the New York Giants the following

week would be a meaningless romp for the Browns, as far as the League standings were concerned.

When the Browns reached the Stadium they found it populated by 31,585 freezing football enthusiasts. The temperature was only 12 degrees above zero, and the field had been kept from freezing only by the tarpaulin that covered it during the night.

The Clevelanders also found a fired-up St. Louis Cardinal team that had posted five victories and a tie in its last six games. Midway in the season, the Cardinals had faltered, dropping games to two second-division clubs. Now, however, they knew they had a chance to win the Eastern title themselves, and they were set to play all-out football.

St. Louis' quarterback was the scholarly Charlie Johnson, who between football seasons did graduate work in a specialized field of engineering at Washington University. Johnson was keenly aware of how much this game would mean to the St. Louis team.

After the Cardinals' mid-season slump Johnson had begun to study football as hard as he studied engineering during the pros' off-season. "You can't get ready in one day," he commented. "Each game is a week-long job." He regularly took home films of earlier games and gave them careful scrutiny.

172

Charlie Johnson, the Cardinals' quarterback, in action.

On this frigid afternoon, Lou Groza scored four field goals for the Browns. He kicked one in each quarter, and saw a fifth attempt blocked by the opposition. His first one covered 22 yards and put the Browns out in front, 3–0.

The next score was one that Cardinal fans will remember for a long time.

All teams in professional football use the primary-and-secondary-receiver type of pass offense. The quarterback has one particular player picked as his first potential target. If that man is too well covered by the defense, the passer has a secondary receiver, or "saver." To make this system work, a quarterback must have what almost amounts to split vision, and he must be able to get rid of the ball in a fraction of a second. It is important to keep this in mind to appreciate the St. Louis play that follows.

As the second period opened, the Cardinals were in possession of the ball at midfield. With third down coming up and seven yards to go, Johnson called a pass play.

The potential receivers on this play were the Cardinals' two running backs, Prentice Gautt, halfback, and Joe Childress, fullback. Childress had just returned to full-time duty after weeks of part-time playing necessitated by a pulled muscle. The play called for Gautt to take the pass after making a token block. But when he saw that the Browns were putting a big rush on Johnson, he switched and headed in earnest for defensive end Jim Houston. The resulting collision flattened both men.

Childress, meanwhile, had burst through the middle of the enemy line and reached the Browns' 26-yard marker. Spotting him there, Johnson pegged a perfect pass. Childress caught the ball and, outlegging defensive back Larry Benz, lugged it into the end zone.

Bakken's successful conversion kick put the Cardinals ahead, 7–3. On the second play after the ensuing kickoff, Cardinal linebacker Larry Stallings intercepted a Cleveland pass to send the Browns into a state resembling shock. St. Louis went on to score two more touchdowns in the second period— one on a quarterback sneak by Johnson and the other on his pass to flanker back Conrad. The extra point was kicked successfully for each, so that the Cardinals were out in front by a margin of 21–3 before Groza kicked his second field goal in the final minute of the period. The score at half-time was St. Louis 21, Cleveland 6.

In the second half the Browns were at a disadvantage. They couldn't run Jimmy Brown, pro football's mightiest ball carrier, as much as planned because they were too far behind. They went into a long-passing game in a desperate effort to catch up.

However, Frank Ryan, their fine young quarterback, could not match Charlie Johnson's throwing prowess in this game. He did fling a 30-yarder for a touchdown in the closing minutes of the struggle, after Lou Groza's educated toe had added two more field goals to Cleveland's total. Before he could do so, though, Johnson himself had engineered another quarterback sneak for his second touchdown of the day. The final score read: Cardinals 28, Browns 19.

175

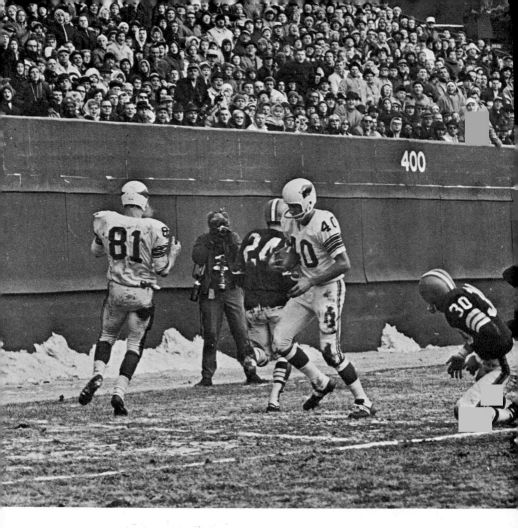

Thus the Cardinals scored their biggest victory
of the season. They forced the Browns to go into the
final weekend to nail down the Eastern title, which
they did by routing the Giants at New York.

The Cardinals, too, won their final game, to wind
up the season with nine victories, the same total
they had amassed the year before. Now Charlie

Bobby Conrad (40) scores a touchdown in the Cards' big second-period rally.

Johnson knew for sure that careful pre-game preparation paid off in handsome fashion.

The Browns had learned a lesson, too. Never celebrate the victory before the game has been played and won. They didn't toast their triumph until, a week later and a thousand miles away, they had earned the right to do so.

177

A Note about the NFL

The first organization of professional football teams came about in 1920. Ten teams got together to form the American Professional Football Association. The group included the Cleveland Indians, the Chicago Cardinals, the Canton Bulldogs, the Massillon Tigers, the Akron Professionals, the Dayton Triangles, and teams representing Rochester, Rock Island, Decatur and Hammond. Jim Thorpe, the famous Indian athlete, was the first president.

The Association was reorganized in 1921, and in the following year it changed its name to the National Football League. For several years it limped along between success and failure, the number of member teams varying between a maximum of twenty-two and a minimum of eight. Then the Chicago Bears signed Red Grange, who had starred as the "Galloping Ghost" halfback of the University of Illinois. He was the nation's most talked-about sports personality. Grange and the Bears went on tour, playing both league and exhibition games throughout the country. Many people saw pro football for the first time and became fans. Attendance at games became larger and more enthusiastic.

In 1933 the National Football League established an Eastern Division and a Western Division, later called conferences. It became traditional for the leading team in the Eastern Division or Conference to meet the leading Western team in an annual playoff game to decide the NFL championship.

NFL football grew more and more popular during the 1930s, developing such great stars as Bronco Nagurski, Sammy Baugh and Don Hutson. Then, after World War II, a new league—the All-American Conference—began operations. It included teams from Cleveland, Los Angeles, San Francisco, Buffalo, Chicago, Brooklyn, New York and Miami. After four season, 1946–1949, the AAC broke up and three of its members—Cleveland, San Francisco and Baltimore—joined the NFL.

Pro football zoomed in popularity all through the 1950s. The NFL roster expanded to fourteen teams with the addition of the Dallas Cowboys in 1960 and the Minnesota Vikings in 1961. The present lineup of NFL teams is as follows:

Eastern Conference	*Western Conference*
Cleveland Browns	Baltimore Colts
Dallas Cowboys	Chicago Bears
New York Giants	Detroit Lions
Philadelphia Eagles	Green Bay Packers
Pittsburgh Steelers	Los Angeles Rams
St. Louis Cardinals	Minnesota Vikings
Washington Redskins	San Francisco Forty-Niners

Index

Index

182

Index

183

THE PUNT PASS AND KICK NFL LIBRARY